W9-ASZ-249

Strange and Unexpected Love

To Lorri

With best wishes—

Tanya G. Heller

Strange and Unexpected Love

A Teenage Girl's Holocaust Memoirs

Fanya Gottesfeld Heller

Foreword by
Rabbi Irving Greenberg

KTAV Publishing House Inc.
Hoboken, New Jersey

Copyright © 1993
Fanya Gottesfeld Heller
Library of Congress Cataloging-in-Publication Data

Heller, Fanya Gottesfeld.
    Strange and unexpected love : a teenage girl's Holocaust memoirs /
Fanya Gottesfeld Heller.
        p.   cm.
    ISBN 0-88125-467-3
    1. Heller, Fanya Gottesfeld. 2. Jews--Ukraine--Skala-Podol'skala-
-Biography. 3. Holocaust, Jewish (1939-1945)--Ukraine--Skala
-Podol'skaya--Personal narratives.   4. Jewish girls--Ukraine--Skala
-Podol 'skaya--Biography. 5. Skala-Podol 'skaya (Ukraine)--Biography.
I. Title.
DS135.U43H454   1993
947' .718--dc20
[B]   93-25613
                                                                  CIP

Manufactured in the United States of America
KTAV Publishing House, Inc., 900 Jefferson St., Hoboken, NJ 07030

This book is dedicated to the loving memory of my parents
Benjamin and Charlotte Gottesfeld

Contents

Acknowledgments

The writing of this book spanned a period of three years. During this time many people and experiences affected my life and consequently the telling of this story.

It was during a UJA Mission to Dachau in 1988, led by Erica Jesselson and her late husband Ludwig Jesselson that I first began thinking about writing this book. Erica and Luddy's deep and abiding friendship has provided me with an important anchor in my life since the death of my dear husband, Joseph. They opened their hearts and their home to me and gave me the courage to pursue this endeavor.

I would like to express my appreciation to several people who offered me assistance, advice and unstinting encouragement. I am indebted to Rabbi Irving Greenberg, President of CLAL for his insightful, thought-provoking and reverent foreword, to his wife Blu for her special sensitivity; to Dr. Arnold Richards and his wife Arlene Kramer Richards for their unfailing perception; to Joan Rosenbaum, Director of The Jewish Museum, for her enduring support and to Helen Nash for her friendship and poignant response to my story.

I offer special thanks to Rabbi Dr. Norman Lamm, President of Yeshiva University, and his wife Mindy for including me as a member of the family of this outstanding academic institution.

I am grateful to Morris Talansky, Executive Vice-Chairman, International Board of Governors, Shaare Zedek Medical Center, Jerusalem. This book has benefitted in a myriad of ways from his many talents. He has generously lent his creative energies to ensuring that my story will be read, contemplated and understood. I thank him for his friendship and his guidance.

Dr. Philip Felig, a great humanitarian and my personal physician, was constantly there for me during the process. He kept me going whenever my anxieties took over and began to manifest themselves in physical symptoms. He believed in this project and helped me through some very difficult times.

I am indebted to those who helped shape the manuscript and bring it to fruition. Anneliese Wagner's enthusiasm, energy and editorial abilities were skillfully applied to molding the material. Nessa Rappaport, Aviva Cantor and Dr. Eva Fogelman provided relevant criticism and praise. I am grateful to Bernard Scharfstein, of KTAV Publishing House Inc., who furnished the final tender touches to the birthing of the book. I also offer heartfelt thanks to Rochel and George Berman of Berman Associates for their untiring efforts to introduce it to the widest possible readership.

I wish to acknowledge the support and love of my children, Miriam, Benjamin and Jacqueline and my grandchildren, Natasha, Adam, Sophie, Shira, Joshua, Aliza, Sarah and Joseph. With this book they have joined me in a painful journey back to the past. I honor the memory of my mother, Charlotte Gottesfeld. Despite poverty and bereavement following my father's death, she made a life and home for my brother Arthur and for me.

Of course, I, alone take full responsibility for my account and for the accuracy of my recollections. Since many of the people I describe did not survive, I can only hope I have recorded their actions fairly. I pray that their spirits will find solace in the knowledge that their experiences will become part of the history of our people. May their memories be blessed.

Fanya Gottesfeld Heller
New York, NY
October, 1993

Foreword

The Nazis laid down their arms and surrendered on May 9, 1945, but their process of inflicting pain and death on Jewry never ended. The continuing casualties can be seen in the higher mortality rates and shortened life spans of survivors everywhere. The pain is renewed in the isolation of people who face an old age of absolute loneliness or who sit *shiva* all alone because many of the relatives or friends who should be with them did not survive. The Holocaust lives on, inflicting wounds, in the nightmares of those who relive moments of painful separation and helpless humiliation. It strikes without warning in the day reveries which summon up moments of agony-filled flight with lungs bursting and heart wildly beating, or eternities of terror (that actually lasted days or hours or minutes) in which people sat, totally defenseless, watching as the heartless death-dealers came closer and closer.

The survivors are the unsung heroes of this relentless war which hatred and death wage against love and life. Since 1945, we have taken them for granted—a sin for which we shall all be held accountable when we get to the *olam ha-emet*, the world of truth.

There was no advance preparation to treat the survivors—so many died during liberation when, in an excess of mistaken good will, they were given too rich food, too much, too soon. There was no world consensus to help them—so many languished in DP camps or in Cyprus detention centers for years. There was no understanding—so many were greeted with devastating suspicion ("What are those numbers on your arm? Were you a criminal, imprisoned somewhere?") or with dismissive coldness ("Why do you *farshter* [disturb] our *simcha* with your terribly sad stories?").

Many survivors fell silent, never to speak again. Others did not tell their story until decades later, when the atmosphere changed, when they could finally trust society enough that it would listen respectfully, if not sympathetically. Yet, despite all this, the survivors went on living; therein lies their heroism and greatness.

Was there ever courage to match their daring plunge back into life? The survivors had to exhibit open-eyed bravery, knowing that no one act of sacrificial abandon, no brief charge into the jaws of hell, would win them victory or blessed surcease from sorrow. To decide to live was to commit to an endless twenty-four-hour-a-day, seven-days-a-week battle with demons of fear and pain who probed continuously for every weak spot to unravel their will to live. Who but the Eternal One can ever measure what prodigious efforts were needed to scale a wall of betrayal, cruelty, and apathy in order to trust another person enough to love again? What steadfastness did it take to grapple with the memories of evil and death that ceaselessly pull the survivor away from the living and back toward the grave? What extra measure of bravery did it take to keep the battle within, without dragging others into the line of fire, in order to live as if life were really normal?

What elemental will-to-life did it take to wrestle all night—and then all day—with Esau's champion and not to yield? Jacob, the mother's boy and trickster, emerged from one night's wrestling grown into Israel, the one who struggles with God and human beings and overcomes. Then what name can adequately describe the stature of the survivor who wrestles all his or her life, who grapples on after being exhausted? after being lamed?

Fanya Gottesfeld-Heller, the author of this memoir, is such a heroine of life and love. As this book reveals, she lived with demons and memories, wounds and torments. Every step that she has taken over these decades has been shadowed by unresolved questions and torturing mysteries. Yet one never would have known this from the daily annals of her life. With her husband, Joseph, she created a new life in a new country. They put behind them the evil past, yet brought with them their background, their Jewish tradition, their commitment to family, their love of good deeds, their creativity, initiative, intelligence, judgment, drive. Together they built a family with good Jewish and human values, a successful business run ethically and responsibly, a career of service and *tzedakah* for many Jewish causes. Fanya took up advanced study and serious analysis as well.

And when she suffered the untimely loss of her beloved Joseph, Fanya did not withdraw or grow disillusioned. She responded to her grief by stepping up her good deeds, her care for others, her generosity and helpfulness, her commitment to life. And now, she has taken up the task of witness and writer. The unfinished story of her remarkable second life is not told in this memoir. But I refer to it because I believe that Fanya and Joseph's life together deserves to be seen in all its heroic stature in the context of the story told here. The life that they lived so lovingly, so beautifully after all that they went through is more than we, or God, could ever have expected or deserved. No wonder the Talmud tells us that God puts on *tefillin;* in the divine phylacteries is written the praise: "Who can compare to your people, Israel? [They are] a people unique in the whole world!"

The tale that is told in this memoir is related in a quiet voice; the book speaks with discretion, understatement, restraint. But no one should underestimate the power and depth of its witness. Scene after scene lacerates our souls and breaks our hearts. Who can ever forget the description of the murderous *aktsia*, the frantic race to hide, the fetid air, choking, being unable to breathe in the hiding place, as the dogs came closer? You will remember grandfather Azriel Gottesfeld, the tall, straight soldier, marching in the front row of Jews, proudly wearing his

Emperor Franz Joseph military medal, then being shoved into the boxcar for Belzec. You will remember Zhenia, who asks to be sent to Belzec to bring an end to the suffering, but is sent to serve as a maid, who is taken by an SS man to be his mistress and seeks to play Queen Esther's role to help save Jews, who is ditched by that same man when he is found out, who is dumped by him in the village square as he shouts "whore" and curses at her; she runs to save her life but is shot down by him in cold blood. Afterwards, the townspeople tear all her clothes off and mutilate the body . . .

You will remember the bystanders: how Stanislaus tears Chaya the Wig's baby apart . . . how Sidor, who was good enough to hide them, makes his move on the young teenage girl, Fanya . . . how the neighbors stand by laughing, cheering, screaming as the Germans, tipped off, search and dig out the barn in which Jews have hidden . . .

There is not a false note in the book. No vaseline is smeared on the lens of this camera which zeros in on all who are caught up in this world. It records unflinchingly: Grandfather Jakob caught by the Nazis, broken by the prospect of death, begging to save his life by turning in hiding Jews. He leads the killers to the place where his wife, among the others, is hiding. The cruelty in this scene could only be topped by the final act. The Germans shoot Grandfather Jakob with the brutally cynical statement, "This is how we repay traitors."

Marynka, Sidor's wife, constantly rages against hiding the Gottesfeld family, constantly threatens to inform the Germans, then flirts with Fanya's father . . . who must not offend her, indeed must pacify her in his responses.

Father and mother, trapped, struggling with despair, cut off from community and calendar. Not even knowing the date of Yom Kippur, Fanya's mother guesses at the date and fasts . . . Father does not.

Father and mother know that non-Jew Jan's love for their daughter has moved him to hide them, to feed them, to save them. In the unspoken interstices of relationship, understanding, judgment, need, they accept and communicate this to their daughter. They (unspoken) know when the relationship turns physical and also (unspoken) resent the embarrassment of a Jewish-Gentile relationship.

What are we to make of the account of the teenage girl and the family's savior? We can appreciate the delicacy and tact of the account; there is neither a haze of nostalgia nor any retroactive whine of the victim. Jan is presented kindly, understandingly, but no roseate halo colors his picture. Can the emotions of gratitude, attraction, caring coexist within one person, side by side with anger, suspicion, resentment? Can a book capture such complex truths without resorting to breastbeating or to Grand Guignol scenes? Read this account and you will experience its integrity and truth and understated power.

Thousands of personal accounts from the Shoah have appeared, but our need to know is not sated. We need more books like this one. We need to know how people lived (and died) humanly during this inhuman period. We need to know more than the mass killings and general roundups. How did individuals adjust, struggle, work, shop, help their families, keep friendships, watch the sun rise? Every scene, every face, every name snatched from the maw of forgetfulness is a victory for memory over oblivion—which is to say, a victory for life and love over death and the void.

We need these victories—and not just to fight the Holocaust deniers and revisionists. (The names of those pathetic liars will be erased by the very history they seek to twist and obliterate.) We need these victories because it is part of our effort to restore the balance of life and memory which was so badly disrupted in the Holocaust. We need them because we are all called to witness. We have always been called to give testimony: "You are my witnesses, says the Lord" (Isaiah 43:10).

Perhaps some will nevertheless whisper: Why tear open old wounds? Why rattle skeletons in the closet? Let the Talmud respond: "Perhaps you [as potential witnesses] will say: who needs all this trouble? Your answer is already spoken [in Leviticus 5:1] 'if he is a witness—he saw or he knew—if he does not tell it, then he shall carry [the stain of] sin upon him' " (Babylonian Talmud, Sanhedrin 37a).

So sacred is the name of God that the *halachah* forbids us to treat it with any hint of disrespect. Thus, pages printed with God's name cannot be thrown away, even when worn out. Known as *shaymos* (names), these sheets are to be buried with respect.

So precious is the human being that he or she must never be treated with disrespect. One who dies must be handled and buried with the greatest of respect. The halachah goes so far as to rule that even articles of clothing or other items that are splashed with the blood of a dead or murdered person cannot be thrown away. They must be reverently buried.

I believe that the halachah already forbids people to handle books like this one except with the greatest of respect. Someday it will be recognized that it is forbidden to throw one away. Even when its pages are worn out from countless readings and endless pondering, such books will have to be reverently buried, for they are written—and suffused—with people's blood.

Irving Greenberg
Jerusalem, Israel
September 21, 1993

Preface

My first session with a psychoanalyst in New York took place in January, 1969. I thought psychoanalysis would be the best way to start the New Year. Disturbing thoughts still possessed me from the days of the Holocaust.

It took two years in therapy before I mustered the courage to tell the psychoanalyst what I had faced during the war, beginning with the German invasion of Poland in 1939, and ending in 1944, when our area was liberated by the Red Army.

This moment of joy was marred by a grievous tragedy, for my beloved father was murdered just as the Russians freed us. His body was never found, though we searched the battlefields.

I still did not wish to believe that the man my family suspected had committed the crime. This was probably the main reason I chose to enter therapy. I wanted somehow to find out the truth.

close by the train is waiting

—PRIMO LEVI

                                          when
Nothing stood between us, we found
a way to come together

—PAUL CELAN

I

Escape

(September 26–29, 1942)

Chapter One

"**T**HEY'RE COMING!" Aunt Lolla shouted.

Thinking myself in the grip of a bad dream, I tried to shake loose, and rolled deeper into the blanket on the floor of the attic. But footsteps clattering on the stairs shocked me awake.

"Run, run fast!" echoed from every room, the panic reverberating through the walls of the stairwell. Doors slammed open as mothers searched in the dark for their sleeping children.

I checked the window, which looked out on the main avenue of our *shtetl*, Skala. Through the early-morning haze I could make out figures in German uniforms two blocks away jumping down from a truck, its headlights dimmed; and closer, men with rifles and machine guns kicking in doors. Huge dogs barked, and several that were unleashed darted in all directions.

It was, I later found out, the beginning of the *aktsia*—the day and a half of September 26–27, 1942, when the Gestapo and the Ukrainian militia coalesced into a single hydra-monster that stalked every one of Skala's Jews.

Our family of sixteen—my parents, younger brother, aunts, uncles, and cousins—had assembled the night before in the home of my mother's parents, Jakob and Miriam Wasserman, a large house with three huge windows from which we could watch for the Germans. After dinner in the living room, we had debated whether they would come for us during the night.

"Not on Succos," one aunt had said.

"That's what they expect us to think," my father said, warning that the Germans had their own ways of celebrating our holidays.

I considered his insistence on a night-long vigil at the attic window an unnecessary precaution, but also knew that his hunches about German actions had always been right. We took turns as lookouts, but as the night wore on, my young cousins straggled off one by one to various bedrooms, and each hour after midnight pairs of uncles and aunts gave up and found beds.

At the first tinge of light, only Aunt Lolla, my mother's sister, and I remained at our posts, and I had fallen asleep. It was Lolla's total obedience to my father's instructions that saved us.

The thud of bodies colliding on the upstairs landing sounded in my ears as I raced out the door without coat or shoes, wearing nothing but my nightgown. I was still in curlers, because after dinner the evening before I had washed and set my hair and tied a kerchief around my head in preparation for today's festivities: Succos and my eighteenth birthday.

I ran toward the hiding place that my father, Benjamin Gottesfeld, an engineer by profession, had prepared for us with the help of my uncles. It was at the end of a huge yard, stretching for the equivalent of more than five or six blocks, owned by Grandfather Jakob, whose lumber business had once been the largest in Skala.

At the far end of the yard stood a villa, a beautiful house Jakob had built for his eldest son, my uncle Wolf. The villa's two back rooms adjoined a warehouse Uncle Wolf had rented out to an egg-exporting firm before the war. It had been taken over by the Germans, and a few Jews were doing forced labor there under guard.

My father, working for weeks at night, had broken into the warehouse through a closet in one of the villa's back rooms, removing the door and camouflaging the entrance with a false panel—an unremarkable-looking wall lined with shelves. Under the floor of the main workroom of the warehouse he had dug a cave for a hiding place. Night after night he had carefully carried out the sacks of earth without leaving any tell-tale trace of what he was doing. He had covered the ground inside the hole with straw, and with the help of my uncles, Wolf, Munio, and Mottel, had buttressed the hole with logs.

Jumping over pieces of lumber in the yard, and tumbling across a rolling barrel, I surged straight ahead amid the noise of screams and shots coming from just beyond the wooden fence. From no farther than a block away, the sound of heavy battering preceded a volley of gunfire. I felt a sudden pain in my shoulder—a bullet must have hit me! Ignore it and run faster, I told myself, but the lumber yard seemed to have grown longer since the last time I had walked through it.

Uncle Wolf and his wife and two daughters had slept in the villa that night, and they didn't know what was happening. My father had knocked on their door to awaken them. By the time I got to the villa, he had gone into the back room—Wolf's room— and removed part of the panel covering the closet. He told me to squeeze through the opening. I crawled into the narrow, very long workroom of the warehouse, which held tables covered with eggs, boxes, egg-candling devices—all the paraphernalia necessary for an egg-exporting business. Then he handed through my eight-year-old brother Arthur and my mother; and after her came Grandmother Miriam, aunts, uncles, and cousins. Only Grandfather Jakob remained in the villa.

Peeking through the camouflage of clothes in the closet, I heard my father shout at Jakob. Tugging at his gray beard and squaring his sturdy shoulders, my grandfather shook his head in an emphatic no. My father gestured toward the entry and finally gave him a shove, and I helped steady him as he came through. He brushed my arm away. What had appeared to be an old man's trembling was instead the bristling of fury.

Standing on the straw and sawdust that covered the floor of the warehouse, with not even a corner to hide in, we were startled by a series of crisp raps on the false panel. For a long minute the rapid blinking of my father's eyes belied the rigidity of his body. A neighbor and her daughter were standing in the back room of the villa, having somehow learned about our hiding place, and insisted on being taken in. Knowing we couldn't risk leaving someone outside who knew where we were hiding, my father opened the panel to let them into the warehouse.

Chapter Two

AT THE FAR END of the room, my father pried a square cutout from the wooden floor and motioned us, one by one, down a ladder into our hiding place. The hole was packed so tight that our shoulders overlapped as we crouched. I rubbed my eyes. I thought I'd gone blind. No, it was simply so dark that I couldn't see my hand when I raised it. My heart, still racing at the pace of my sprint across the lumber yard, clanked and expanded beyond my ribs and seemed to speed toward a crash. My father whispered that we must not speak.

My Aunt Malcia stopped a few rungs down the ladder and held out her arms. Her husband, Uncle Wolf, placed their fever-flushed five-year-old daughter into her arms. "Diphtheria," my mother whispered. The sick little girl began to whimper. "Sleep," her mother crooned, "go to sleep."

I don't know how long it was until we heard footsteps above us, the unmistakable tread of heavy boots mixed with lighter footwear. Aunt Malcia put a gag in the child's mouth as we held our breath. I worried that they'd see the outline of the trapdoor of our hideout in the sawdust as they scoured the place, but somehow my father had managed to disguise it with straw. The crack and splinter sound of breaking wood I was listening for did not come. The Germans had orders not to destroy the warehouse, which had become German booty.

"No Jews here," I heard someone call out, and another voice echoed his report. "Bring a dog," someone ordered. I held my breath as I heard a barking creature rampaging above my head. But the smell of broken eggs must have confused him. Eventually, the Germans and Ukrainians gave up. A few curses at Jews and they left.

Someone needed the chamber pot. Suddenly we all seemed to need it. There was none. My father had barely finished building the hiding place and hadn't had the time to enlarge it or stock water and food, and this was its trial run. No pot, no water, not even a candle, and almost no air.

Despite the heated squeeze of bodies perspiring from running, from crowding, from fear, I began to shiver. Only the damp, compacted clay I felt as I reached my hands above my head calmed me, reassured me.

One thing left to do: I began unrolling the curlers from my hair. I didn't want to be caught with curlers in my hair when they came back to drag us out. I'd often tormented myself with the scene of my last moments: What would I do? Beg them not to shoot? Would I cry, wet myself as I was doing right now? They wouldn't shoot us in the yard, I kept assuring myself, not in my grandparents' yard. I know that if I cursed them to their face they would. And I'd heard shots as I ran. Where would they take us? To the cemetery? At that moment I heard a train's whistle. They had sent a train for Skala's Jews.

In the crush of the hiding place, gasping for air, with the feverish child's moans an accompanying baseline, suppressing as long as possible the need to relieve myself again, I wished at one moment that they *would* come, find me, drag me out and get it over with. And then, seeing how selfish that thought was—it meant that seventeen other people would die too—I took back my wish.

In the jumbled hours and minutes of that day and then annexed to the interminable night that followed, only specific moments mattered: the release of a leg from its cramped twist or the shift to hold Arthur on my lap to give my mother relief.

Arthur, though small for an eight-year-old, squirmed a lot and had to be soothed to sleep. Feeble snores told me the sick child was still breathing.

Efforts to breathe rasped all around me. We pulled the same fetid air into our lungs and pushed it out again. Once in a while, when someone fainted, my father tilted the cover up for a few moments and the person was held up for a few fresh breaths, but the risk was great. If a looter was rummaging about, he would surely betray us.

I slept. I slept through most of the second day.

Chapter Three

A FTER HEARING the train whistle, my father climbed out of
our hole and went to the attic of the warehouse to see what
was going on. It looked quiet, but we waited another day before
he went to the attic to check again. He seemed to be gone for
ages.

"All quiet," he reported upon returning. He knelt at the edge
of the hole and held out his hand toward us. "It's over."

We sat there. After a while I got up and helped my father pull
the others out of the darkness. I tried to steady them against the
light. My grandparents sprawled on the floor of the warehouse,
and the children jumped around a bit.

We crawled back through the closet into Wolf's villa and
walked into the front room.

We heard the door open.

On the doorstep stood a six-foot-tall young Ukrainian militiaman with armband and rifle.

There was a moment of terror.

Then we saw he was "our Jan," the man who had befriended
my parents, brother, and me in the past year of the German
occupation, who was in our house practically every day bringing
us food and news, the man my father had trusted with the

knowledge of our hiding place. "Our Jan," who was called a "Jewish uncle" by his compatriots, a derogatory and insulting epithet meaning "Jew-lover."

Without putting down his rifle Jan hugged and kissed me and Arthur and my mother and father, and we hugged and kissed him.

"It's over," he said again and again, "it's over." Jan had been hanging around the villa for hours, waiting for us to come out. He was afraid to go in, fearing to be spotted and followed by a passing militiaman. All of them knew how he had protected us in the past and had scorned him for it.

My mother began to cry, and seeing her, I felt in danger of doing so myself. No, I thought, I'm alive, why cry? I kissed my Grandmother Miriam, and she squeezed me lightly. Her usual strong bear hug had fled. Grandfather Jakob stood near her, his body taut, and I tried to take his hand, but his fingers remained rigid and I let go of them.

The family split up. Wolf and Malcia and their daughters stayed in the villa. My grandparents went home with Uncle Munio and Aunt Suza, who lived with them. The four of us and Aunt Lolla and her husband and two sons set out for the house we shared, with Jan accompanying us.

What we saw on the way was a scene out of Dante's *Inferno*. Dead and dying people were strewn all over the street. Children were running around looking for their parents, and parents were looking for their children. Houses stood empty as if a cosmic cyclone had sucked their occupants to another planet. There were dead bodies lying on the beds and floors. The doors and windows were smashed open, and everything was gone—clothes, furniture, all the occupants had possessed had been taken either by the Germans or the Ukrainian militia or by Polish and Ukrainian looters.

The doors of our own house, down the block from my grandparents', were broken and the glass from the windows was lying in shattered pieces. Everything in the house was gone. The only thing left was some photographs, and they were strewn all over the floor, pried out of their stolen frames. There was no food; the little hiding place we had kept it in behind the wood panel of the wall in the entrance hall had been discovered.

Jan brought us a bit of food and milk for Arthur and Lolla's boys and stayed with us the rest of that day and all that night. We were afraid to go out to get water and didn't wash.

He told us about the *aktsia*—how the doors were smashed with poles and axes, and Jews routed from their houses and from bunkers and hiding places, beaten and humiliated and some murdered on the spot if German commands were not instantly obeyed. They were stripped of any valuables they carried or had hidden in their clothing. The sick and mentally retarded were shot. The others, shoved, clubbed, their heads cracked open, were herded to the *Umschlagplatz*, the assembly-point at what had once been the Polish officers' garrison on the main avenue and from there to the barracks once used by the Polish border guards, now surrounded by a barbed-wire fence. When the Nazi count, taken at noon on the second day, fell short of the expected 700 dead or captured, several members of the *Judenrat*, or Jewish Council, and the *Ordnungsdienst*, the Jewish auxiliary police unit that enforced its decisions, were added to the complement of prisoners. Only one was able to buy his way out.

Jan reported that a conductor had told him that the young and able men were taken to the Janowska camp in Lvov. A man had jumped off the train and told everyone the destination of the old, the women, and the children: the Belzec death camp.

Chapter Four

THE DAY AFTER THE *aktsia*, posters went up in Skala ordering the 700 Jews still remaining there to go to the ghetto in Borszczów 15 kilometers away. My parents hired a man with a cart to take them and our Wasserman grandparents and Uncle Wolf and his family to Borszczów. The drivers who returned reported that Jews from several towns were stuffed together in designated houses, ten or fifteen to a room. Skala was now rid of its Jews—at least as far as anyone could see. Only a few managed to stay on to work for the Germans.

"So where are *your* Jews?" someone had asked Jan on the street.

Arthur and I hid in our house until nightfall, when Jan came by to take us to the barn adjoining his family's house, a ten-minute walk from our home, and we climbed up the ladder to the attic.

Anticipating the need of a hideout for us, Jan had spent many nights in the attic building a false wall indistinguishable from the real one. In the narrow space between the false wall and the real one, he had put a straw stool, an all-purpose hook, and a shelf, and made an indentation in the hay to serve as our bed. There was a chamber pot in the corner.

Jan sat at the small triangular window, an air hole, actually, since it had no glass. He was watching for activity from the house. His mother, sister, and brother-in-law, who lived there with him, though sound sleepers, could have caught a glimpse of our arrival. His mother had forbidden him to bring us to her place, and his sister and brother-in-law had taken him aside and told him that they would turn us and him in if we were found on the premises.

Jan told me that my father's widowed father, Azriel Gottesfeld, had been shoved into a boxcar of the train bound for Belzec. He hadn't had the heart to tell my father about this. "There's time tomorrow," he said.

I loved Grandfather Azriel, who had bought me chocolates and other treats at the Cukernia café when I got A's in elementary and high school. In his youth, Azriel had been a soldier in the Austro-Hungarian army. His height and carriage and handsome beard had so distinguished him as a model of manhood that he had been chosen to stand in the front rank when Emperor Franz Joseph reviewed the troops. When someone betrayed to the Germans the hiding place he had built for his son Leo, and Leo's wife, Laura, and their daughter, and himself, Azriel had walked to the train in newly polished boots, as well-groomed and proud as when he had been a young soldier. He took with him only his *tallis*, his prayer-shawl.

That night, seated on fresh straw in the attic hideaway of Jan's barn, I burst into tears. With Jan there I felt safe; my weeping had to do with the warmth of the blanket, the sweet aftertaste of bread in my mouth, the hay that still carried the summer meadow in its scent, the news about my beloved Grandfather Azriel, and my exhaustion from two days below ground waiting to be discovered.

"It was my eighteenth birthday and we were eighteen people in there," I said to him. "What do you think it means?"

"It means you're alive and so are they."

I moved closer to him. "For a while down there I didn't know if I was alive or dead." I was sure I'd been shot while running in the lumber yard, sure for days that there was a bullet poking my shoulder blade like a giant needle.

Jan began to twist and turn me around for signs of a bullet hole. His fingers looked through my hair for evidence of my being grazed. "Nothing," he said.

"But I felt the bullet enter my back as I ran. It's in there. I can feel it."

He searched me again. "Don't think about it now." He said nothing more and smoothed his hand over and over on my hair. Then he leaned back and pushed the brim of his cap over his eyes.

That night it seemed as if I couldn't get enough of the moonlight, and I fell into a dream of gentle winter snowfall, the snow as white as the moon.

II

Growing Up in Skala
(1924–1941)

Chapter Five

SKALA, THE *shtetl* where I was born on October 14, 1924, means "rock"; the old city was built on a rocky hill surrounded by a small forest and situated on the river Zbrucz, which had a little beach. The surroundings were so beautiful that there was talk before the war of making it a resort area.

Before World War I, Skala had been part of the Austro-Hungarian Empire. After it was ceded to Poland in 1919, the river became the border with the Soviet Union and Skala became a garrison town, with about four officers and fifteen soldiers quartered near the marketplace. They rode about on horses and spent most of their time drinking, playing cards, and womanizing.

The town had 5,500 inhabitants. About 3,000 were Greek Orthodox Ukrainians; 1,000 were Catholic Poles; and 1,500 were Jews, the vast majority observant, including our own family.

Our relationship with the Poles and Ukrainians was always strained. The peasants were superstitious and still believed in the blood libel, and the priests told them again and again in church that the Jews had killed Jesus. Sometimes when they drank too much after returning from church, they threw stones at Jews or beat them, and we always closed our windows when we saw them coming up the street.

We knew little about the gentiles; they lived their lives and we lived our lives.

Business was the main contact between us. There was a marketplace on the main avenue facing my Wasserman grandparents' house. At least twice a week, the Ukrainian peasants would bring their produce—eggs, beans, grain—to sell there to Jewish merchants, who exported these commodities to Western Europe and elsewhere. After the market they would go to a *kretchma*, a little inn, to drink. The Jews would be standing on the avenue, one after another, outside their little stores located in the front rooms of their homes. The peasants would come out of the inn to buy kerosene, salt, sugar—which was very expensive and sold in lumps—fabric and clothing, hardware and farm tools, and leather.

There were also occasional fairs where the Jewish merchants went in carriages to sell the peasants suits and other clothing they had made, and boots, shoes, and quilts. Our only other contact with the Ukrainian peasants was when we needed them to be *shabbas goyim*, to light the stoves and ovens on the Sabbath. Once a year, on New Year's Eve, the Polish officers held a big ball at their garrison, inviting only the "fine Jews"—my father, my mother, and her beautiful younger sister Suza among them.

The Jews in Skala knew one another so well that they spoke of each other not by name but by nickname—the *shtume* ("one who doesn't speak"); the *krumeh*, ("someone who couldn't stand up straight"); the *sauer* ("sour one," someone who was depressed); "the wig" (a woman who had lost her hair and wore a bright red wig).

We had a very rich social and cultural life centered around our two-story Bet Am (community house). It had a large auditorium where lectures and concerts were held, an amateur theatre troupe performed, and where we celebrated Purim and Chanukah and other holidays; a library with 5,000 books; a reading room; and a very high-level Tarbut (Hebrew cultural movement) school which ran from kindergarten to the eighth grade.

The situation in Poland after the First World War was difficult

for Jews, but it deteriorated even further after the death of
Marshal Pilsudski, a socialist whom the Jews looked to as their
protector, in 1935. The Jews cried bitterly when he died—they
knew what was coming—and shortly after, the fascists took over
and implemented official anti-Semitic policies, hoping to forbid
ritual slaughter and instituting an economic boycott of Jewish
enterprises.

Jews felt they had no future in Poland, and many—including
a second cousin of mine—became Communists or Zionists. We
had an active chapter of Jabotinsky's Revisionists, religious Zionists, and pioneering movements that sent young people on *hach-
sharah* to training farms where they prepared for *aliyah* (immigra-
tion) to *kibbutzim* in Eretz Israel. Hashomer Hatzair, Betar,
Hanoar Hatzioni—all these youth groups met in the Bet Am.

Chapter Six

M Y FATHER, Benjamin, was the third of the nine surviving children of the thirteen born to Azriel and Hinda Gottesfeld—and was his father's favorite. Azriel came from a very poor family and worked as a glazier; he had golden hands. He built a hothouse for the wife of a Polish count who liked him, and later he built his own family a beautiful two-story house on a main street across from the Polish garrison. He had tenants in the upstairs story and in the basement.

Azriel was very tall, good-looking, and proud, and carried himself like the soldier he once had been. He was also the kindest human being, very good-natured and sweet. He and my grandmother Hinda, a very smart woman, always ate from the same bowl, and he helped her bake the bread when she was pregnant or nursing and busy with the children.

Mendel was their oldest child, and after him came Esther. She married a boy named Mendel Gottfried, who had left Skala for Paris, where he set up in business importing eggs from Skala. He did very well there, but returned to Skala to find a bride. He and Esther brought five of her brothers and sisters—Mendel, Usher, Krenia, Brana, and Tuvia—to work with them in Paris. Esther and the others sent money to their parents, and Azriel used some of it to set up a small hardware store. He never forgot that he had been poor, and every Friday gave needy Jews potatoes, flour and bread, and *matzah* for Passover.

Every year Esther took her parents to a spa. She and the other children used to visit them in Skala in the summer, and this was always a major event for us.

From Paris they brought grapefruit, oranges, chocolates, and the best sardines, and left us their clothes before going home. They hired a cook for their summer visit and invited guests for dinner. Hinda didn't like my mother, who she felt was making too many demands on my father for a higher lifestyle than he could afford, and the only time she invited us over for some cake was when her children came from Paris. Otherwise, she never had us over for meals, and I never slept at their house or had a relationship with her.

Azriel and Hinda's three other children—Leo (Leibish), Sophia, and my father—remained in Poland. Leo became a very wealthy and successful businessman in Lvov, but returned to Skala after the German invasion.

Sophia was an intellectual who knew *Tanach* (the Hebrew Bible) and quoted Bialik's poetry by heart. But she was not considered marriageable because she did not live up to conventional standards of good-looks: fair, pink, and plump, with beautiful hair and full breasts. But because of the money Esther and the others sent their parents, there was enough of a dowry for her to have married a doctor or lawyer, about $1,800 by the going rate. She married Zygmunt (Zisha) Zimmerman when she was twenty-four—then considered an advanced age for a girl's marriage—and they had a son, Dolek.

To the end of her days, Grandmother Hinda never forgot how worried she had been about Sophia. Even though she no longer had daughters to marry off, she was jealous of parents whose girls had married "young." She would comment to my father, "Nu, some people have luck." My father would reply, "Mama, you've married Sophia off already, why are you still jealous?"

Chapter Seven

MY MOTHER, Szencia (Charlotte), was the daughter of Jakob and Miriam Wasserman. Already a rich man from the lumber business when he was still young, Jakob could afford to marry Miriam Horowitz, a Bukovinian beauty with no dowry. Miriam had big blue eyes, and was good-natured and resourceful. Jakob gave her a very lavish lifestyle—many servants and a *drozhky*, a carriage with horses to take her to market. She wore lovely Victorian-style suits.

The house they lived in on the main avenue of Skala was magnificent, with high steps at the entrance, large windows, beautiful furniture, and heavy velvet drapes, dark red and green in color. Grandmother Miriam had a large garden where she grew tomatoes, strawberries, raspberries, and cucumbers as well as flowers. There was a gazebo in the garden where we'd have coffee or cold drinks on Shabbat afternoons in the summer.

None of our homes had electricity, and the rooms were heated with coal stoves. Our drinking water came from a well, via pail and rope, in the Wassermans' garden. Water was also delivered from the pump well down a rocky hill where the non-Jews lived—near the Jewish cemetery, the bathhouse where the men went to *shvitz* on Friday, and the *mikvah* (ritual-immersion facility)—by water carriers who sold it to their customers. Once a week, on Thursday night, we heated the water on the stove and brought the bathtub into the kitchen to bathe in. Sometimes I took a bath with my mother in the tub inside one of the little cubicles in the *mikvah* before she went downstairs to immerse herself in the pool, and I'd wait for her until she came upstairs.

But my grandmother had a special bathhouse which Jakob had built in the garden to satisfy her wishes when they were still wealthy; it had a large bathtub. She also had a very nice outhouse with special paper (the rest of us used cut-up newspapers).

Jakob's lumber business prospered until the Depression, when he lost everything and was left with stacks of IOU's. He used to take me up to the attic to show me the sacks of Polish money, which had been devalued and was worthless. They kept the house but had to let the servants go. Jakob was an angry and depressed man, and when I watched the way he drank his tea in the kitchen, elegant pinkie extended, stirring it with a rough twist of the wrist so that some of the liquid spilled, I sensed something troubling, perhaps unsavory about him. Grandmother Miriam's loyalty, her uncomplaining adjustment to the huge diminution of their fortune, spoke to me more forcefully as a model of conduct than Jakob's brusque, sometimes unkind manner.

Although we lived one house away from the Wassermans on the same avenue, and I, their first grandchild, spent a great deal of time in their home, I never saw a smile from Grandfather Jakob, and he never asked me how I was and what I was doing. He often came striding to our door to ask me to write business letters for him to his creditors—my handwriting pleased him—because he couldn't afford a secretary. At Christmas time, he commanded me to deliver cakes Grandmother Miriam had baked and other gifts to his non-Jewish creditors. I treated him the way he treated me: as an honorable business acquaintance. Grandmother Miriam indulged me sufficiently to make up for any lapses of warmth on his part.

My mother was the second of their five children. Wolf was her older brother, and Lolla and Suza were her two younger sisters.

The youngest son, Bubcio, died of galloping tuberculosis when he was twenty-one. Grandmother Miriam had taken him from one sanitarium to another and to doctors in Vienna, to no avail. I remember Miriam sitting on a stool and crying, and I kept asking what had happened—I was four years old and they didn't tell me until much later. My grandmother never recovered from Bubcio's death and always wore black blouses, skirts, and dresses. Her deep, exclusionary mourning for her favorite child was seen by some as exemplary piety and by others as unhealthy behavior. Her great show of grief was balanced by Jakob's stoicism.

Wolf was the apple of my grandmother's eye. He was the intellectual, he had studied in a Polish *gymnasium* (high school), which had a quota for Jews and was extremely expensive, and then at university. He was very religious, he recited poetry, he could give nice speeches; but he had no profession and couldn't make a living, so Grandfather Jakob had to support him. Then he married Malcia, a rich girl from another *shtetl*, near Stanislaw, about 70 kilometers from Skala, and they had two daughters. Malcia was a little older than Wolf and was considered past her prime, but she had a dowry, which they lived on. She also had a little business crocheting lace curtains, which she ran out of the small villa Jakob had built for his son.

My mother's younger sister Lolla was very beautiful—with light eyes and reddish-brown curly hair and a full figure. She was very vain; I always remember her with a mirror in hand. She liked to dance, sing, and go to parties, and was very popular. She was also an intellectual and was always reading. Although she had graduated from the Polish teachers' seminary, she never wanted to work. She married Mottel Feingold, who was her intellectual inferior but had a very good business selling shoes, bags, and sweaters, and he was on friendly terms with the few Polish noble families in town. They had two sons. The oldest was Julek, who had flaming red hair. He was a good boy and tried hard to please his mother, but she didn't like him and he never got any affection from her. The youngest was David, who had beautiful blond hair and blue eyes. She loved him and took him from doctor to doctor because he was sickly.

The youngest sister was Suza. She was blond and blue-eyed and very tall, statuesque in her long dresses. She had a beautiful voice and was a singer in the amateur Hebrew and Yiddish theatre troupe which performed at the Bet Am. All the Polish officers chased after her, and it was Suza who attended their New Year's ball in a long evening dress.

By the time Suza was of marriageable age, eighteen, Jakob had lost his money, and she knew she wasn't going to have a dowry. She decided to learn a profession and take care of herself. She went to Cracow, where Grandmother Miriam's well-off sister lived, and learned at a trade school how to make corsets and bras. She opened a very elegant little workroom in her parents' home, where she made all the corsets for the officers' wives and the noble ladies.

Suza loved Munio, a dentist from Czortkow, about 40 kilometers away, and everyone knew about their relationship. One evening I found them lying together under a blanket on the living-room sofa at our Wasserman grandparents. This kind of behavior was considered improper—our family was rather prim—but it intrigued me. It seemed like something out of the novels I'd been reading.

Chapter Eight

M Y FATHER WAS very handsome; he had gray eyes and black hair, and was generous and kind like Grandfather Azriel. A good man with a good heart, he would often send some poor person to my mother and instruct him to tell her, "Your husband said to give me a coat."

Although the family was poor when he was growing up, my father went to a Polish *gymnasium*. He supported himself by tutoring other students at the *gymnasium*, and his parents sent him food packages. By the time he returned to his room from the post office with the package, he had eaten all the crackers, he was so hungry. After *gymnasium*, he studied engineering at the university in Czernowitz, but nobody needed a civil engineer in Skala. He started a little hardware store which went bankrupt because he let customers buy on credit.

He had courted my mother for five years. Szencia was beautiful: she had dark eyes and black hair, and beautiful white teeth. Although she had attended a business school in Czortkow, she wasn't really interested in her studies and, unlike Suza, never tried her hand at a career. Instead, she took over the family housekeeping. My mother called herself the Cinderella of the family because after they had to let the servants go, she did all the chores, including cleaning up after Lolla. She accepted the explanation that her father had been cheated by a junior partner rather than believe that the state of the economy and her father's inability to cope with it had caused the loss of his fortune.

Despite having lost all this money, Jakob was opposed to my mother's marrying my father because he came from a poor family. My father threatened suicide, and the Wassermans finally gave in, but Grandfather Jakob refused to give my mother a dowry because she had married my father against his wishes.

Jakob bullied my father to give him the little money he had left after the hardware store went broke, and my father became his partner in the lumber business. He lost everything and there was a falling-out between the two men, which accounted for the surplus lumber which lay, for years, piled in our yard. My father took the blame for the failure of the partnership, saying he was not a businessman, and steered clear of his father-in-law. Later, he started a small lumber business in his own yard, where I used to hide and read my books.

My father had no head for business; he was a scholar, a man of the *Haskalah* (Enlightenment movement), a believer in education who loved literature and loved *Yiddishkeit* (Jewish culture). He was part of the small intelligentsia in Skala whose members came to our house to play chess and cards and discuss politics and current affairs. They included the commander of the Polish garrison, the postmaster, the manager of the estate of Count Golochowski, the principal of the Polish elementary school (a rabid anti-Semite), a rich landowner who came to my father for advice, a man named Ulanowski who was a member of the Polish *Szlachta* (gentry), and Moizesevich, an Armenian, who owned the only pharmacy in town. I used to go to his beautiful old pharmacy with its dogwood, jars and scales, and fantastic smells, to pick up medicine for my parents.

Our home was full of books in several languages—French, Russian, German, Polish, Hebrew, Yiddish. When I was a little girl, my father would hold a book in his hands and I would trace the words as he read. Sometimes the book had no pictures, but I didn't care. His voice, the resonance of it as it came into my back, my hair, my ears, filled me with comfort, and sometimes

I stopped listening to the words and just held on to the sonorities of sound.

My father wanted me to be educated, but my mother didn't care. She was not an intellectual, and her passion was being a *balabusta*, a meticulous housekeeper with the reputation of having the cleanest home in Skala. She wanted me to get married, and worried that I wouldn't because there was no money for a dowry.

Chapter Nine

I RECEIVED MY primary education at the Pulaski School, a Polish
institution, every day until 1:30 p.m. The school was free, but
it was not obligatory, and a large number of the peasants never
sent their children there. Classes were held on Shabbos, but the
Jews didn't go and the Polish pupils used to tell us what
homework had been assigned. While in elementary school I
wrote an essay for a contest sponsored by a savings bank on why
people should save money. Uncle Wolf helped me with the essay
and I won first prize.

Each ethnic group in the school had religious instruction once
a week from its own special teacher. The Catholic priest taught
the Poles; Father Derewienko, the Orthodox priest, taught the
Ukrainians; and a Mr. Bouk instructed the Jews. Mr. Bouk was
an old bachelor who lived with his two unmarried sisters. We
didn't take him seriously and used to play, eat, and write letters
during class. I would read my Polish books.

One of my fellow pupils was the grandson of the manager of
the count's estate, which was his summer residence, located near
the railway station and a small forest, about a 20-minute walk
from the center of town. As children, this boy and I played hide-
and-seek in the estate's huge and beautiful park, which was

replete with lawns, statues, lakes, gigantic trees, and a lovely garden. His family would invite me at Christmas to see the tree, and I was entranced with the glass balls, the lights, and the angel on top. But typical of our relationship with the gentiles, we never invited them to our home for Chanukah.

In addition to the Pulaski School, I went to Hebrew school from 3:00 to 6:30 four afternoons a week and all day Sunday. On Sundays in the summer, Hebrew school classes would often go to the little forest near the train station for lessons and a picnic.

The school was part of the Tarbut movement, and our teachers, who had all been educated in the movement's seminary, were very dedicated. There was a strong Zionist atmosphere in the school. All the subjects—Jewish poetry, literature, and *Tanach* with Rashi's commentaries—were studied in Hebrew, and it was also the language used in our special projects and plays. I loved Hebrew school and thrived on the work, using the huge school library with much gusto.

One of my distant cousins, Choneh Gottesfeld, who had gone to America and become a writer, returned to Skala to visit his parents. Everyone thought he was a famous writer, and the Hebrew school held a special assembly where he spoke to us and asked us questions, and we sang songs and recited poems. I was chosen to deliver the paper I had written on the Marranos—in Hebrew, of course. (When Choneh returned to America, he wrote a book in Yiddish about his visit to Poland.)

For an hour in the late afternoon after Hebrew school we went to the home of Sluwa Kassierer to do homework under her supervision. Sluwa and her two sisters, all of them seamstresses, supported their old parents and lived in two small rooms. They were close to thirty, and their unmarried state was considered a *shanda*, an embarrassment. Every family who could afford a few pennies considered it proper to send their children to the Kassierers to do their homework. Actually, we didn't do much there—we usually ate apples and socialized.

After eighth grade, I wanted to go to high school, but there was none in Skala. Fifteen kilometers away, in Borszczow, there were a state high school, with a quota for Jews, and an expensive private school. A lawyer manqué named Lachmann organized a school in Skala in a rented room for a student body of twelve, covering the first two years of high school on the strength of his brilliance as a teacher of math, history, geography, and literature. My father had once wanted to send me to Hebrew high school in Stanislaw, but this never materialized, so after Lachmann's sessions from 8:00 a.m. to 1:00 in the afternoon, I continued at the Tarbut school. The teachers determined the curriculum for the higher grades and essentially taught what they wanted.

The tuition for both schools, which was high, came from Grandfather Azriel, who was interested in my education and had also paid for Hebrew elementary school because my father didn't have the money. Azriel came to our house every Saturday afternoon with a gift of chocolate and asked what book I was reading. Whether Polish or Hebrew, I'd tell him its story or recite a poem for him. He was the first person I went to whenever I got a good grade. When Lachmann gave me A's, Grandpa Azriel took me to the Cukiernia, a coffee house, for currant drinks and ice cream with waffle-wafers.

Once in a while I stayed overnight at my Wasserman grandparents' house—usually a Sunday night. I engineered the sleepovers when I was engrossed in a particularly long novel—Dickens or Tolstoy—so I could read all night long and stay in bed with the book Monday morning instead of going to school. Sometimes, when I was reading at night by the light of a candle, Grandfather Jakob would catch me and warn that I was going to go blind or crazy from too much reading.

In the morning Grandmother Miriam would bring me hot chocolate and sit on the bed steadying the tray. "Reading is bad for the eyes, and who's going to marry a girl who wears glasses?" She reminded me that I wouldn't have much of a dowry. I'd tell her I wasn't interested in marriage, and she'd reply that this was all the more reason to leave school and apprentice myself to a steamstress.

My two grandmothers, who differed on just about everything else, agreed that sewing should be my livelihood—and the sooner the better. In Grandmother Hinda's view, advanced schooling was a waste of time and money for a girl and had the potential to

Chapter Ten

LOTKA AND ZHENIA were my two best friends from elementary school on. Lotka and I were second cousins; her grandmother and Grandfather Jakob were brother and sister. We lived next-door to each other, with our house on one side of hers and my Wasserman grandparents' on the other, separated by a little garden.

Lotka's parents, Mottel and Szencia Sternberg, were among the few Jews in Skala who did not keep a kosher home. Their cook, Lotka once told me, used to prepare ham and fry pork chops in butter. In the 1930's, Mottel had lived in Prague. Upon returning to Skala, he married Szencia, and they opened a very fancy grocery store in the large front room of their house, patronized by the Polish officers and the town intelligentsia. I used to be entranced by the chocolates and jams and fancy cakes, and sometimes Lotka shared a package of French butter cookies with me. Even if I wasn't her cousin, Lotka had said when we were little, she would have chosen me as her friend.

Lotka was beautiful, with brown hair, green eyes, and heavy, dark eyebrows like her father's; and she played the violin. I always thought .myself ugly in comparison to Lotka and was jealous because the boys I liked ran after her, not me. I had a crush on our classmate Rubcio, but he preferred Lotka. He liked me as a friend with whom he could discuss books and issues, but it was Lotka he wanted to hold hands with and kiss. The Sternbergs considered him an inappropriate boyfriend for Lotka because his parents owned a *kretchma*, an inn where country people in town for a fair or a trip to the post office—people who would never think of shopping at the fancy store the Sternbergs owned—stopped for a drink.

Rubcio lived in one dark room of a house on the main avenue with his mother, whom I always remember peeling onions to add to the herring for the peasants, his father, an old-maid aunt who washed laundry for a living, and two orphaned child relatives. The other three rooms constituted the *kretchma*.

Szencia wanted me to be Lotka's friend so that I'd be a good influence on her—encourage her to read and study, and help her with her homework. I admired Szencia for her cosmopolitan tastes; she was well-read and sensitive and easy to talk to. She was the first person who told me I had beautiful eyes. This was something I'd never heard from my father, who always told me I was smart. My mother had never taken me aside to point out any good features, although she once admitted that I'd inherited my father's intensity and ingenuity. When Lotka's mother, while Lotka and I were still in Lachmann's school, told me that I had beautiful eyes, I became quite swell-headed for a time. I saw Lotka as my rival for her mother's praise.

Zhenia was my closest friend and, secretly, my alter ego. Zhenia was radiantly beautiful; she looked like an angel. When I recognized her face years later in reproduction of a Fra Angelico painting, I soon realized that I had taken her fair skin, bright blue eyes, curly hair, and red cheeks as the standard for good looks. As we entered our early teens, her body filled out and mine simply elongated, making my movements jagged as I walked while hers seemed like a dance.

Zhenia's mother was a homely woman, an orphan who had been an "old maid" when she got married. She had been engaged to my father's brother, Leo, who left her to marry Laura. Leo was plagued by acute headaches, perhaps induced by guilt for leaving his first fiancée, that drove him to seek help from doctors in Vienna. The man Zhenia's mother married died of a heart attack when he was still young. Zhenia, her mother, grand- mother, and uncle lived together, with the grandmother support- ing all of them from her *kretchma*.

An only child, Zhenia had a sense of herself as selected for special privileges, and when she managed to advance from grade to grade without any effort, she took it as her due. I never saw her read a book in all our years together in Polish and Hebrew school. She didn't care about her studies and was a vivacious, happy-go-lucky type. Zhenia seemed under the wing of a super- natural protector. If she stole a handful of cherries or apples from a neighbor's tree or tomatoes from someone's garden, no one noticed; but let me stretch out my hand to pluck a fruit and a stone would strike my hand.

Zhenia and I devised many carefree activities, such as the foolhardy climb up sheer rocks in unsuitable shoes for a view of the river near the Turkish Tower, the ruins of a thirteenth- century castle. The Tower looked mysterious and romantic, especially at night by the light of the moon. Only young people went there—it gave us a sense of freedom to run from the ruins of one hall to the other. I used to walk up to the Tower with Lotka, too, and with my first boyfriend, Izio.

I had met Izio on the beach where some of us used to go to sunbathe or to swim in the river. He was ten years older than I, and this impressed me at the age of fourteen, as did his having served in the Polish Army, smoking cigarettes, and looking like a non-Jew. My parents and Aunt Suza commented on our age difference, saying, what does an "old guy" want from you? I impressed him, he said, because I spoke beautifully. We used to meet secretly on the promenade above the river and go walking there on Sunday afternoons. He held my hand, he wrote me letters, and several times we kissed each other.

In September 1939, Izio was called up to the army. War had broken out. I went with him to the train station to say good-bye.

Chapter Eleven

THE RED ARMY marched into Skala in mid-September 1939. The Polish soldiers and officers, taken by surprise, tried to run away, clad only in their underwear, but were taken prisoner.

Some of the rich people in town managed to escape, among them Count Goluchowski, who drove off to Romania in his car. (He later lived in Palestine and then settled in England.) The Russians occupied his estate and established a hospital there. Some Jews also ran away, fearing they would be sent to Siberia. Lotka's parents fled with her to Lvov, which was, of course, also occupied by the Russians, but since it was a large city they hoped to get lost there, something impossible in a small *shtetl* like Skala. Many Jews from German-occupied western Poland had also streamed to Lvov and other cities in the eastern part of Poland taken over by the Soviets.

The Jewish Communists in Skala embraced the Soviets the same way the Ukrainians later welcomed the Nazis—with a great feeling of exhilaration. One of my father's cousins, had been a leader of the underground Communist party and was imprisoned and tortured in Bereza-Kartuska, the infamous prison for politicals, where his fingernails were torn off. When the Russians invaded eastern Poland, he was freed, and he returned to Skala a great hero. He became a big shot in the Russian administration, got married, and had a child.

It was a benign occupation at the outset. The Russian soldiers had been instructed to propagandize among us, and although we spoke no Russian, we could understand it a bit, and they understood some Polish and Ukrainian, as related Slavic languages. They used to boast that their factories could produce anything. I remember one girl asking a soldier whether they had lemons and he answered, "Of course, our factories *make* lemons!"

The Russians closed all the stores and warehouses, and the peasants robbed and looted them. The Jewish merchants and storekeepers lost everything and became impoverished overnight. Every man became an employee of the state, working in agriculture, the stone quarries, or on road and rail construction.

My father, assigned to work as an engineer, was put in charge of repairing the bridge over the Zbrucz River, which had been damaged in the early days of the war. I often brought him a hot lunch at the bridge.

It was during this time that he met Sidor (Isidore), a Polish peasant who was to play a crucial role in our lives three years later. Sidor was working in the labor brigade on the bridge, and at one point, when he didn't fulfill his work quota, he was accused of sabotage. My father, who was known for treating the workers fairly, intervened on Sidor's behalf and saved him from punishment. This was something Sidor never forgot.

My father also had a little black market business going with some of the Russians, supplying them with leather hides they sent home to make boots with, for which they paid in gold coins. He and other Jews in town had saved and hidden some of the hides they had acquired before the war, and these later came in very handy in bartering for food and other necessities and for bribery during the German occupation.

One of the Russian officers who bought some of my father's hides used to visit us frequently, and after a few months he admitted he was a Jew and showed his passport to prove it. Stationed in Skala among all the Ukrainians and Poles, he'd seen too much of what happened to Jews, even Jews who wore a Russian uniform, to admit it earlier. He would drink vodka from a large glass, and sometimes when he was drinking he'd cry. One time he spoke of the Bolsheviks, who, unlike the Mensheviks, he said, were not against the Jews, and of how the Jews had joined their ranks.

One Friday night, my mother served him tea in a glass in a silver holder. That was a signal that he was a special person, someone to be nice to. She offered him some of her cherry preserves and a cake she'd made. While he ate, he cried. I can still see his streaming tears, the runnels of tears flowing into his mouth as he took one bite after another. The peaches and cherries my mother had preserved in brandy reminded him of his family, the times of plenty and then the times of killing and dispersion. All of his family had been transported to Siberia.

Crying and eating, the sugar and salt mingling, he looked up and said, "You don't know how good you have it, such a good life." He grasped a large glass of vodka and swept the arm holding it to take in the room, furniture, food, and the four of us without spilling a drop. Then, with one lift of his elbow, he downed the vodka. Realizing, perhaps, that he had gone too far, he looked around the room as if totally sober at that moment, then took another piece of cake, stopped crying, and began to sing.

Chapter Twelve

U NLIKE THE POLES, the Russians had no objections to Jewish students attending a state high school. Since Skala had no high school, I went to the one in Borszczow after passing the entrance exams. My mother paid for my room and board with a Jewish family—Mrs. Bradler, her daughter Rose, and a son-in-law.

I was fifteen, and this was my first time away from home. I remember sitting on the bed in my rented room before the semester began to sew the school insignia on the breast pocket of the jacket which I was to wear over a dark navy jumper, the school uniform. The insignia had an ascendant eagle and a motto about a mighty mind and a lofty soul.

As I knotted the final thread, I thought about how little of myself I revealed to others, how my book-world often seemed the ultimate reality, and that I needed something more challenging than a small-town milieu to pit myself against. Sitting with the blazer on my lap, I ran my hand over the lettering and the eagle, and a slight twinge of fright mingled not unpleasantly with the lure of the unknown.

Most of the students in school were Jewish, but there were a few peasant youths, plus all the sons and daughters of the

Russian officers. The Russian students knew little of the outside world. Once, when we were discussing art, someone mentioned the Louvre, and a new Russian student asked, "The Louvre, is it in Borszczow?"

I gave all my attention to my school work and to trying to fit in with my classmates. I veered between timidity and acting the eager beaver, switching back and forth according to my guess about what the teachers demanded.

The Russians had gotten rid of the pictures of Jesus and the Madonna and Child that had once hung in the classrooms and replaced them with portraits of Stalin. They had also fired all the Polish teachers and brought in Russian replacements. History was dropped, and the geography of the Soviet Union and the history of the Revolution were taught instead. Latin was also excised from the curriculum.

All subjects, and of course, Marx's and Lenin's writings, were taught in Russian, the official language. We were forbidden to speak Polish or Hebrew; and many works of world literature, and of course, Polish literature, were forbidden as well. We had a lot of physical activities and calisthenics, plus military training with rifle practice, taught by a Russian officer, handsome as a movie star, whom all the girls, including me, had a crush on.

The teachers frequently demanded that we write our autobiographies. When describing my family, I mentioned only Grandfather Azriel, who was a glazier. I ignored Jakob's existence since he had once been a well-to-do merchant. I struggled with myself over omitting Jakob, since not naming him implied a sort of death, but I could think of no way to protect him other than to deny his existence.

The teachers started to make young *Komsomols* out of us. I came to believe strongly in the socialist principle that by working together people could produce what was needed and would receive an equal share of what was produced. Being a *Komsomol* meant having to go to meetings all the time, trying to earn medals for achievements, and giving one day of labor a week. On Saturdays, to earn medals, I shoveled snow, worked in the fields, or taught peasants who were brought to the school how to read and write Russian. We also worked in a public health clinic where we would talk to the peasants and hold their hands while they were getting vaccinated. On my first working Shabbos, I feared that God would punish me for breaking the Sabbath, even that He would take off my hand, but He didn't seem to notice.

One of the literature teachers, a tough woman commissar, wore the usual uniform of collarless blouse, long skirt and high boots, and no make-up; and her hair, the same color as her wan skin, was combed tight against her head and anchored down. Ten medals rode bronco over her restless bosom. She never allowed a lesson to pass without commenting on my hair, which I wore in a page-boy that glanced off my shoulders as I walked. Long hair, she said, took time away from study or useful work, and how could I be a *Komsomol* if I spent so much time on my hair?

Eventually, I simply pinned it under, or rather, Stasiek, a Polish boy who sat behind me, would fold and secure the thick coil until it resembled a strap of black leather. The touch of his fingers as they grazed my neck tingled in a way that made me look forward to that class and dread it at the same time.

If it wasn't my hair, the teacher found something else with which to ridicule me. She gave frequent oral exams; to spite her, I didn't do the homework, and when she called on me, I spouted answers written on my hand. Heat rose to my cheeks and up through my head so that at the roots of my hair I knew the consequences of sin.

It was this same teacher who called me in and wanted me to denounce Grandfather Jakob, whom they had obviously found out about. He was rich, she said; who is he, does he have servants?

How could I denounce my grandfather? I said; Look, I don't know anything about him, I don't have any relationship with him.

The principal told us that it was our duty to reveal the names of members of an organization at school who were "enemies of Russia." This was a group of Ukrainian students my own age who had secretly banded together. After they were caught and forced to "confess," they were shipped off to Siberia and none ever returned. Their faces haunted me.

Once all the students were ordered to watch the public execution of a black marketeer in the market square. The man was already starved and beaten to death when they brought him there in a truck with a sign around his neck reading I'm a Traitor. All the stores were closed—it was like a holiday—and the workers, together with the students, were made to watch the noose being placed around his neck. When he was hanging, we were told to applaud. One of my girlfriends, Irena, almost fainted, and I kept holding her up. We applauded, and the man was left hanging there for four days. When I had to pass the square on the way to and from school I was terribly frightened.

Chapter Thirteen

THOUGH BUDDING YOUNG *Komsomols*, my friends and I practiced minor deceptions. My friend Shimek (Samson) would give us passages from outlawed Polish books, which we circulated and discussed among ourselves. And we laughed when Galsworthy's works were forbidden but Gogol's were not.

Sweet, brilliant Shimek Bosek had been my friend since I was a young girl in Skala. His father and mine were best friends and had studied together at the university in Czernowitz. Mr. Bosek came from a fine family, some of whose members had settled in Paris, and his brother, Mendel, was a violinist.

Shimek's father was a Zionist who had settled in Palestine in the 1930s. But he had suffered from malaria and the unsettled conditions and had become disillusioned. Returning to Skala, he married and opened a little store. Shimek was an only child.

Shimek and I had gone to elementary school, Polish and Hebrew, together, but he was two years older than I, so when I was at Lachmann's school, he was already attending the high school in Borszczow. By the time I entered the lower grades of the Borszczow high school, which required a blue emblem on our uniforms, he had advanced to the higher grades, where the insignia was red, and it was his old emblem that I sewed on my blue jacket.

In the winter of that year of high school, when we returned home on visits, we held gloved hands while dragging our sleds up the hill—each the other's consolation on the hill of adolescence—and then descended the slope alone, each sitting singly upright or slung belly-down across a single sled.

In the spring, when the weather was fine, Shimek and I would often sit in my parents' garden talking about an absorbing book. Brilliant Shimek! How I admired his ease with languages! To dazzle me he'd switch from English to German to Latin to Hebrew in one sentence.

At dances, though, Shimek was no help; he didn't like to dance. I did and would scan the room for a partner. The experience of looking for a dancing partner reverberates in my memory as my most absorbing interest at the time, eclipsing for the most part rumors that somewhere west of Skala our enemies were preparing an invasion.

Shimek and I were offered a chance to study Russian in Leningrad. We were thrilled at the prospect of becoming interpreters. Our fathers feared that two young Jews in a big foreign city would end up in Siberia. The night I discussed this with my father, he suffered a violent ulcer attack, which settled it for me. Shimek decided that if I was not going, neither would he.

On one of my visits home from school I learned that Grandmother Hinda had died, and on another visit, that Suza and Munio had gotten married. They went to a rabbi in Czortkow 45 kilometers away instead of having their wedding in Skala, and did not invite her parents or sisters. When they came back from Czortkow, Grandmother Miriam gave them a little party. I also found out that the Soviets had closed the synagogues and the Hebrew school, and had confiscated most of the books in the library. Several Jews had been deported to Siberia.

I remember endless journeys in winter darkness from Skala to Borszczow and back, with me squeezed in a public sled between Russian army personnel. There was always one who had an "illness" my girlfriends referred to as Roaming Fingers. The fierce cold stung my face while waves of heat singed my body under the heavy traveling rugs. The Russians laughed at my protests or accused me of "wishful thinking."

I remember one soldier, as he removed his hand, sputtering, "Freckles! A girl with freckles! What man would want you? Why don't you buy some cream and get rid of them?" Another said, "With your figure you should wear trousers," and his friend stuffed a cigar in my mouth. The sled drivers, who were Jews, ignored me. I never mentioned any of this to my parents, but in bed at night I'd vow to report my tormentors, only to lose my resolve by morning. The next time it happened I froze and burned as usual.

In the last year of high school, I experienced curiosity about love and sex as private excitement, as day dreams and shy crushes on boys or as puppy love for the officer who gave us military training. I was still seeing Izio, who wrote to me at school and once in a while visited me there.

I thought my dark navy jumper helped bring out the midnight-blue tints of my hair. Since my body was just beginning to find its curves, I had to count on my coloring—almost-white skin and faintly Oriental gray eyes—for the promise of good looks. On asking my mother whether I was pretty she had said: "You have the look of a smart girl." Grandmother Miriam mystified me further with the caution not to look "serious," that it was unbecoming in a girl. People did respond to something in me: perhaps the *joie de vivre* one of my Parisian cousins had once mentioned in a letter after a visit or a type of gumption that someone else had labeled naiveté and was simply the perky openness of adolescence.

It would not have occurred to me that Jan, ten years my senior, would notice me as I returned home from Borszczow one day and then on numerous other days; would notice particularly the insignia on my school uniform, and be able to describe the eagle in detail years later during the times he held me in his arms for hours on end to lessen my fear of the guns beyond the door.

III

Under the German Boot
(Summer, 1941–
September, 1942)

Chapter Fourteen

J UNE, 1941. I had finished two years of high school in Borszczow and was home on summer vacation when we heard the
news that the Germans had marched into Soviet-occupied Eastern Poland. The Soviets abandoned Skala, and its warehouses
and stores were looted by criminals and Ukrainian peasants. My
Communist cousin joined the fleeing Russians with a few other
comrades, leaving behind his wife and child.

Two weeks later, on July 8, 1941, Skala was occupied by the
Hungarians, then allies of Nazi Germany. The Hungarians
descended on us like locusts—raping, pillaging and stealing.
Even the loaf of bread my mother had in the oven was stolen by
the Hungarians as they swept through town.

In the last week of July, Hungary expelled the Jews from the
Trans-Carpathian region of Ruthenia, which it had annexed in
1938 when Czechoslovakia was dismembered. Mercilessly, they
drove them across the Zbrucz River toward the Soviet Ukraine.
One day it took hours and hours for 3,000 weary, hungry
Hungarian Jews of all ages, dressed in their best Sunday clothes
and laden with packages, to stumble through Skala.

I saw an old woman beaten by a guard with a club until she
bled—it would have been suicidal to run and help her. A guard

stood there swigging from a bottle and pointing his rifle at her. Finally two men further along in the column dragged her with them as they passed. Later, I was told about the boy from Ruthenia who had appealed to the soldiers for food and rest and was hung upside down in the town square. Every time he fainted, water was thrown over him. A Skala rabbi came to pray at the scene until the soldiers beat him unmercifully. Finally his sister, a girl I knew from Lachmann's school, managed to bribe them to stop.

The Jews of Skala collected food and clothing for the Hungarian Jews and bribed the soldiers to allow them a brief rest in town. They brought hot food for all and medicine for those beaten by the guards and Ukrainian peasants, and rented wagons to take the Jews the rest of the 20, 30 kilometers to the Ukrainian border.

Jews who had fled east in 1939 a skip and a hop ahead of the Germans after they invaded western Poland had told us their horror stories of internment, confiscation of property, brutality and murder. "Exaggerations," is what most of us preferred to believe when we heard these tales. The Germans, according to my father, had a tradition of enlightenment and he counted on it to mediate the ruthless impulses of the conquering army. This is how denial worked even after reading *Mein Kampf*. For a while it was *if* it arrives. Soon it was *when*.

On a brutally hot day at the end of July, we heard the German Army approaching with their motorcycles and trucks, and ran to hide in Grandfather Jakob's cellar. Looking through the little barred window facing the courtyard, we saw the Germans pitch tents in the lumber yard. The victors jumped from their motorcycles and sidecars and shed their jackets as they lounged against my grandfather's stacks of lumber. After gulping from a jug of milk, one German began to sing a ditty and the rest picked up the refrain. A large blue jar of white cream passed from hand to hand. As grease glistened on their faces and arms, which they tilted from time to time for optimum bronzing, their buttons, buckles, visors, glasses, shiny boots, even their hair and fingernails took on a dazzling sheen like thousands of prisms reflecting the light of Hades' fire. I knew this glitter spelled night and death.

While they bantered and bellowed, their guns and gear spread over territory that had been ours, I knew I wanted to live to see them grovel for mercy on the dirt of the yard, their faces glistening from the sweat of fear.

From the cellar window, we could see the Ukrainians—who wanted an independent state and believed the Germans would give it to them—welcoming the conquerors with blue-and-yellow Ukrainian flags and swastika armbands. Father Derewienko, the Greek Orthodox priest, greeted the Germans with the traditional gift of bread and salt.

The entire night before the German's arrival, our dachshund, Ralf, had howled and cried pitifully. We couldn't find him when we ran to hide in the cellar and when we came out from there, we went to look for him. We found him lying dead in the garden. He had not been killed—he had just lay down and died.

We buried him in my grandmother's garden, among the flower beds.

Chapter Fifteen

THE GERMANS SET UP headquarters of their civil administration in the beautiful house on the Count's estate. The Ukrainians constituted a militia which the Germans, who had no intentions of allowing an independent Ukrainian state, used to do a great deal of their dirty work—which they did willingly.

The militiamen were all peasant boys who found it glamorous to carry a rifle, put on an armband, lord it over the Jews, and loot at will—and then get drunk and sleep it off. They got enormous satisfaction from thrashing people, including children, and forcing them to cower on the ground before dragging them to headquarters. Many times they shot fugitives on the spot.

Primitif, a popular word in everyone's lexicon, referred to Ukrainians. Even before the Germans' arrival, some young Ukrainians had on whim tossed a grenade into the home of David and Rosa Herscher. Rosa was killed. The few Ukrainians who were members of the town intelligentsia were not known as friends of the Jews. (Ulanowski, whom my father considered a "prince" of a man, was a Pole; Moizesevich, who loved our family, was an Armenian.)

It was the Ukrainians who supplied the Germans with a list of 15 Jewish leaders who were ordered to meet and chose a seven-man *Judenrat* (Jewish Council), whose unenviable job it was to announce and carry out the German decrees. The *Judenrat* was located in the home of Rabbi Yehuda Drimmer on the main avenue. His half-sister, the daughter of his late father (also a rabbi) with a second wife, was a good friend of mine from Hebrew school, two years older than me.

The *Judenrat* was forced to establish an *Ordnungsdienst*, a kind of auxiliary police armed only with clubs that compiled lists of people and property and made sure orders were carried out. My Uncle Zygmunt, Sophia's husband, was a member of the *Ordnungsdienst*. How my father managed not to be conscripted for the *Judenrat* or its *Ordnungsdienst*, I never found out. He was a loner; perhaps he convinced them he could do more good in an unofficial way with his vast network of gentile acquaintances.

One of the Germans' first decrees was that Jews had to wear a white arm band with a blue Jewish star. Within a few days, the Germans ordered the Jews to turn in their radios. Then they demanded Jews deliver up all their valuables—furniture, linens and china to furnish their headquarters—and jewelry.

My father hid all the silver from our dining room cabinet—a set of tea-glass holders, a few glasses for Shabbos wine, our six schnapps cups, our candlesticks, the box where we kept the precious lumps of sugar under lock and key, and some of the cutlery. He buried these objects near a tree by our outhouse in the garden. Most of the silver cutlery remained in the house in a strongbox hidden under the false bottom of the bedroom armoire.

Frequently I had to deliver a donation of linen or china or kitchen utensils or furniture—once the nightstand from my parents' bedroom bumping in a wheelbarrow—to the *Judenrat* to fulfill a German demand. Later, in the dead of a brutally cold winter, a call came down through the *Judenrat* to bring in all fur articles. I delivered the lining of my father's coat, my cowskin muff and Arthur's ear muffs. To disobey was punishable by death. Nevertheless, we hid my mother's Persian lamb coat, hoping to barter it for food.

Sometimes the Germans took hostages to make sure their demands for goods and provisions were carried out. If delivery did not occur within the designated time—two hours, for example—the hostages were shot. Three members of a *Judenrat* committee figured out each family's financial ability so that a tax could be set and the proceeds used when the Germans demanded blackmail money.

The *Judenrat* was forced to register all Jewish men between the ages of 16 and 60 and supply a certain number to report every day to repair the bridge over the Zbrucz River, which the Russians had blown up as they retreated, and to work on the Count's estate and in slave labor camps outside town. Uncle Wolf, forced to work in the fields of Count Goluchowski's huge estate, told us that almost all of the German guards behaved in a barbaric manner towards Jews and only a handful showed humane inclinations. Major Braun, for example, invited Shimek's Uncle Mendel to play violin duets and did not mistreat him, but he never restrained any of his men from beating other Jews.

Daytime now became a menace, a time when my father was in danger of disappearing in a forced labor round-up. For a while, he and other men evaded the daily work groups to escape the brutality of the guards but it meant that the members of the *Judenrat* and the *Ordnungsdienst* bore the brunt of retaliatory beatings. The *Judenrat* was trapped between the community's distrust of their decisions and the orders of the Germans.

Once, when a conscripted group of 50 men that was to go to Czortkow encountered a returning group and learned about the back-breaking work accompanied by beatings, half of them fled. The *Judenrat*, though warned by the Gestapo that hostages would be killed if it didn't produce the escapees, ignored the warning and on that one occasion nothing further happened.

Chapter Sixteen

E ACH MORNING HAD the feel of a starting line on an obstacle
course: no one knew what hurdles the day would present as
we stood poised and waiting, calculating how to preserve our
bodies from the whack of clubs and the bite of bullets.

Thursdays, the worst day of the week for me, meant carrying
buckets of water to fill the bathtub for the week's baths. Jewish
water carriers had been conscripted to perform forced labor so
we had to lug the water ourselves, as we had done under the
Russians, who abolished the water carrier trade. The pump well
designated for use by Jews was 20 minutes away and besides
lugging the full pails home, pumping the handle called for well-
muscled shoulders. On deep winter days when the water turned
to ice and I came home with empty buckets, my mother's
distressed shrug hurt me more than the weight of full buckets
would have done.

My mother seemed to have a premonition that we would not
be living in the house much longer and insisted while she was
still the mistress of it that it look its best. She rubbed and
scrubbed, swept and beat the rugs with renewed energy, folded
and refolded the one extra sheet we owned and brushed the few
items of clothing we still had, then hung them at measured

intervals on the closet bar. Even before the German invasion, she'd banished my father's books to the attic, calling them dust collectors, much to my delight since it was a joy to carve a fragrant nook for myself up there with Heine in hand and apples just an arm's length away, each one laid out separately on rows of pans so that no rotten fruit would infect another. Now there were no more apples and the books collected dust undisturbed by my father or me.

One day the inner door handle, which was protected by a crocheted glove, banged into the chest beside it, fell off, then danced on the floor. Standing in the doorway was Engel, a German officer who liked to be recognized as the lord of the town, the owner of each person and object. You could hear Engel coming because his dog barked and snarled at people as they made their way down the street, causing them to scream and him to curse.

My mother saw how intently Engel stared at me while the dog strained toward her. Even daring to address him before he spoke could risk a bullet. She began pulling a chair towards herself as a shield. He shoved the chair at her with enough force to knock her down.

The dog looked ravenous. He bucked and sprang into the air, the leash still wrapped around Engel's hand. "Very clean," he said. With extended finger he tested an upper shelf. "Clean Jews," he said as if he had discovered a blue rose. He studied the contents of the highboy, as if he might consent to ship selected items in it and the highboy itself home to Juterborg while the dog growled louder by the minute.

I stood there desperate for something to appease the thrashing dog when Engel dropped the leash and the dog's fangs penetrated my side. Engel called him back with words of praise and they left.

My mother tore my blouse off and began washing the wound. She didn't say a word, didn't even ask if I was in pain, didn't hug me or kiss me as she usually did when I was hurt. Both of us were not the same people as we had been half an hour before.

Finally, as she tied a clean dishtowel around my midriff, she asked his name. "*Engel, Engel*," she repeated, not saying a name, nor the German word but "angel" in Yiddish. "Angel, angel, an angel came for a visit."

Chapter Seventeen

THE GERMANS FORBADE the peasants to sell any food to Jews, and it was practically unobtainable as the winter wore on. Once in a while I'd hear a rumor that a farmer had slaughtered one of his animals and I'd take some item from the house in hope that a trade could be made. I'd console myself when I failed that the following day I'd find a way to obtain some flour, buy it or barter for it—or steal it if I could figure out how.

Each day the scramble for a little food occupied me totally. I ran all the errands because my father had to stay off the street lest he be dragged off to a slave labor camp and my mother certainly couldn't trust seven-year-old Arthur to ferret out food. She herself stayed home out of fear that Arthur would fall under Engel's boot if he made another surprise descent on the house.

On one of my errands, I caught a glimpse of Izio—he was, I learned, living in a smaller village about 10 kilometers from Skala, passing on Aryan papers. Other times, I'd see my old schoolmate, the estate manager's grandson, on the street. He'd see me and walk away without saying anything. He kept his eyes on the ground so he wouldn't have to look me in the eye.

Running errands was dangerous. One day I managed to slither past Captain Hera, Braun's deputy, just as he was about to strike

me. Instead he grabbed an old man by the beard and beat him
with his pistol butt. Another day Feiffer, also an officer, stopped
me as I was bringing a pair of shoes to one of my aunts and took
them. He didn't strike me—that wasn't his practice—but he
cursed me on seeing that the shoes were all I had.

Unable to tag after me any more when I left the house or to
wander about outdoors, and small for his age, Arthur created a
place for himself under the kitchen table and like an only child,
he became his own best companion. He played war games,
concentrating on naval battles fought with pots and pans and
crockery. My mother's penchant for a neat house gave way to his
games. I never observed him long enough to determine if the
Jews or the Poles or the Russians or the Germans were winning.
Sometimes the French joined the fray because France was where
we wanted to be: in Paris with Aunt Esther.

Arthur was intrigued by his name, which he associated not
only with the port at the end of the Trans-Siberian railroad but
also with the fortress-like synagogue in Skala called "Port Arthur," built during the Russo-Japanese War. One time he heard
a girlfriend of mine, who had been dragooned into working for
the Germans, say she had made up a package of food from Engel
to send to his family in Germany and that his first name was
Arthur. "No, it's not," Arthur said. She insisted it truly was the
Nazi's name but Arthur shook his head and pounded the meat
mallet on the overturned coal bucket to simulate aerial attack
until we retreated to the yard.

"Oh, go read a book," I hissed at Arthur when one of his
incessant mock battles tangled him around my ankles as I crossed
the floor. "I don't know how," he said, and I stopped for a
moment and tried to think what that must mean for him. I had
read books and discussed them with Shimek, had consumed
knowledge like bread portioned out by my father along with the
daily soup. But Arthur had only completed first and second
grade in the Russian school before the German invasion and he
could barely read.

Arthur was playing on the floor the time Hera and a few of
his men burst in to look our things over. Hera ignored us and

simply pointed to a credenza here or a vase there, which his underling noted in a little book. Hera chatted with one of the soldiers: "Clean, very clean. Reminds me of my mother's house. You could eat off her floor." The other man nodded appreciatively as if that prospect appealed to him.

The men carted boxes of my father's books from the attic and spilled them over the kitchen floor. Hera's anger at seeing volumes of German poets and a set of Nietzsche in a Jew's library drove him to a fit of frenzy. He trampled the pages underfoot, ripped the covers apart and ordered the books destroyed.

My mother faded backwards toward the wall but my father, tears running down his face, stepped forward to retrieve a book. Hera hit him over and over with a torn volume, the jagged edge cutting into my father's cheeks and forehead. "Jew-pig," he said, "now books bring tears, soon it will be your children."

Suddenly Arthur piped up: "Fi, fi, fight him." One of the soldiers aimed his gun and I sprang in front of Arthur.

Hera pointed to some things he wanted his men to carry out. When only one bed, a table and a few chairs remained, he shouted, "Now give this place a real cleaning," and cracked his baton across a dish to demonstrate what he meant.

After they left, while my mother washed the blood off my father's head and I salvaged some isolated pages, Arthur tried to ask my father why he hadn't hit Hera back. None of us were in the mood to remind him of the guns.

From that day on, Arthur stopped playing war games.

Chapter Eighteen

WE HOARDED the little bread we obtained by bartering and every scrap was divided and assigned by size before we put it in our mouths.

Hunger made us desperate. Some nights my father or I would sneak into the fields of wealthy peasants outside town to root for potatoes or beets or cucumbers or to steal rotted pears or apples—anything to stave off our hunger pangs. Sometimes I chewed the stems of the rotten fruit to give my tongue the illusion that food lay on it.

One day we heard a rumor that some peasants had made a delivery to the market. Cucumbers. We'd had nothing to eat for breakfast or lunch and I couldn't remember when I'd last sat at the table and eaten my fill.

I rushed off to the market with my school satchel and wedged myself into the stampede of people to get near the sacks on the peasants' wagons. I tried to press through the crowd by turning sideways and leading with my elbow but I slipped on the slime of the trampled vegetables that looked more like over-ripe squash than cucumbers.

As the sour smell of rot wafted toward me, I heard a woman pushing her way out of the melee say, "It's not worth getting killed for. They're spoiled. The peasants wouldn't feed them to starving cattle." The vegetables were so rotten that the peasants had taken a chance on disobeying German orders not to sell food to the Jews.

With my satchel high on my shoulder, I forced my way between two men. One gave me a sideways kick that caused me to buckle at the knees. I pushed on, not caring if the cucumbers weren't good. My mother would pare away the bad parts. I wished they were potatoes, but cucumbers would do.

"Hey, you with the school satchel. . . ." A tall man with a rifle and wearing the armband of the Ukrainian militia came towards me.

A rush of things to say clouded my brain: "You don't mean *me*" or, "I'll give you some cucumber salad," anything to distract him and not lose my place in line. Instead, I just held out my hand to give him my coins. He closed my hand over the coins and took my satchel. I noticed that his ring and pinkie fingers were missing; the two knobs where knuckles and fingertips should have been looked forlorn.

"Go home," he said in a voice used to giving orders. Then he smiled and I saw that he had even, white teeth. "Go home," he said again but this time his voice had turned soft.

At home, an hour later, my mother happened to glance out the window and saw a man coming to the door. When he knocked, her expression said, I'm not going to open up. Another knock. I rose from my reading to open the door but my mother's trembling hand turned the handle first.

"Here's the cucumbers," the man said. "I'll bring some better ones another time."

My mother held out a coin for him but he waved her away. "I'm Jan," he said as if that explained everything. He took his handkerchief to wipe the cucumber goo stuck to my satchel. "Meant for notebooks," he said.

He looked at me and saw my finger trapped between the pages of a book. "Is it a good story?"

"Yes, very good."

At the door he promised to bring eggs in a basket, not rolling around the bottom of a satchel.

"You have a plucky daughter," he said to my mother. "Bye, Blacky," he called, referring to my hair, since my eyes are light gray.

My mother asked if I knew him, while her fingers were busy pressing the yellowed cucumbers for firm parts. She was too absorbed to see me shake my head. They were lousy cucumbers, ones that had lain in the September field too long: flaccid, bloated things, with parts nibbled away by field creatures or rotted by rain. In better days, my mother would have thrown them in the garbage. I remembered how she used to sort through cucumbers to find small unblemished ones to make pickles.

"I thought you said there were no cucumbers."

"No, I said I couldn't get any," I replied. "I guess I did."

When my father heard about our windfall he nodded, saying he knew the man, that he'd sold him some lumber a while back. "A big man, right? Has black hair and eyes to match?" Jan had stopped him the other day. Scared him half to death: a militia-man. He thought he was going to be taken to join a forced labor gang. "He's engaged," my father said. "Wants to barter food for some linen, cutlery, maybe the Persian lamb coat. I told him to come any time."

We didn't have to wait long. One evening Jan came by our house with his fiancée, the daughter of a wealthy Ukrainian peasant named Dzisiak. She had blond braids pinned to the top of her head and a tightly-wrapped full bosom. Though I'd just begun to "round out nicely," as one of my aunts put it, I yearned to approximate the buxom bride-to-be.

My father went to the bedroom to get our silver cutlery out of the strongbox and my mother carried the silver knives and forks in tissue paper to the table and unwrapped them, lingering for a moment cradling one handle, then rubbing the ornate monogram with her thumb. The bride-to-be weighed each piece in her hand. The wrong initials didn't dismay her but a missing fork did.

Jan sat down next to me. He asked if I missed school. And he wanted to know, while looking straight into my eyes, what I wished my studies to lead to. Medicine, I told him, I was going to go to Paris to study medicine. After the war; my father had promised me. Jan seemed pleased. "Yes," he said, "Yes, Paris."

My father came back at that moment and repeated, "Paris," and then a soft, drawn-out "Paris." In a time of hunger and perpetual menace, at the far rim of Europe, each of us carried a Paris of our own in our imagination. My father steered Jan to the corner of the sideboard and poured our last drop of schnapps for him.

After the engaged couple left and we were sitting at the kitchen table drinking blackberry tea made from leaves I had gathered in the forest the week before, my mother said she didn't trust him, that he was a *goniff*, a thief like all Ukrainians. He had seen what we had left and would come back with a gang of militia who would help themselves and take us away. No, my father counseled, this one was different: "I have a hunch he's a decent guy." My father's hunches were always right, but this time I too doubted him. To me, Jan looked like all the other Ukrainian policemen carrying their ever-present rifles.

Chapter Nineteen

O UR PRECARIOUS EXISTENCE became the central issue at somber sessions my uncles and aunts held around our kitchen table. Each one had a tale of woe to report. When I appeared, they'd gesture with an elbow, a tilt of the head, as if to say, not in front of the child. Some horrors were whispered when I was out of earshot. Soon that pretense fell away.

I was no longer a child. I was seventeen. That fact did not escape notice. My figure had rounded out in all the right places. Jan came to the house several times a week now. "Be nice to him," my father said. My mother baked special cakes for him from the flour he brought us. "Be nice," my father said. When he said it several more times I began to wonder what he meant. I *was* nice to Jan, same as to any other guest.

Dollars and gold coins suddenly began to surface in town. My father managed to convert whatever goods we had left into $250 in fives, tens, and singles, and some gold coins. The American bills were greasy and torn, and he stood in a corner of the kitchen with a pot of glue in his hand, piecing them together and pressing them smooth with the old iron which gathered heat on top of the stove.

We began to notice Ukrainian peasants walking around town in beautiful clothes, high-class jackets and coats in the Western European style.

Then three Hungarian Jewish boys turned up in Skala, the last survivors of the unfortunates who had been herded through town in July. The 3,000 Hungarian Jews, they told us, had been held by the Germans at Orynin. Then they were told they were being sent home but were led to a field and murdered by machine-gun fire. The Ukrainian militia had aided the Germans and were in the front rank of the looters. The boys had wormed their way out from under layers of bodies.

After they told the *Judenrat* what had happened, the community arranged to help them. One family gave them a place to sleep, and others fed them; they ate meals every day with a different family. One boy ate with us one day a week. He was so scared, he hardly said a word. (Eventually, the *Judenrat* got the boys false papers and arranged their escape to Hungary; they all survived the war.)

A few days after we had learned about the horrible and almost unbelievable disaster that had befallen the Hungarian Jews, Jan came to visit us. I was "nice" to him, as my father had suggested. I sat down next to him and complimented him on his new jacket. The fabric, a nubby wool, and the elegant cut with a pleat in the back looked odd over his baggy pants. When I asked him which tailor had made it, he said, "I bought it from a friend."

One day, a peasant came to my father with an American hundred-dollar bill to ask where he could exchange it. We'd never seen such a large bill before.

Jan agreed to go to Czortkow to try to break the bill. He returned with *zlotys* for the peasant and a sack of cornmeal for us. My father invited him to share our meal. Jan took the chair near mine, and sitting next to me became his place at the table from then on.

I found out that he came from a long line of farmers, some of whose descendants still worked on farms and some of whom had moved to town. He had been employed by a shoemaker, hadn't wanted to own his own business.

"How did you pick shoemaking?" I asked him.

"I like the smell of leather." He told me that he had a keen nose, that from me he detected the scent of a lemon tree. I reminded him that he had never smelled a blossoming lemon tree; he knew what one smelled like from the taste of lemons, he said, and I had the same flavor. Just as sour, I teased, and he answered, teasing me back, no, just as shapely.

"I like working with my hands," he said. "It frees the mind. And besides, I can hammer my anger away. Give me leather, nails, and a hammer, and I'm happy."

Jan regretted having left school after the eighth grade, but it had not been his choice. When his father died, he had to support his mother and sister and keep the family farm in good condition.

It was clear that he had the intelligence and skills to be more than a shoemaker. He was certainly not made to be a policeman for the Germans.

It was now us he watched over every waking moment.

Chapter Twenty

THAT COLD WINTER, coal was scarce, kerosene for the lamp down to a trickle, the food shortage severe. My mother's Persian lamb coat had been bartered to Jan's fiancée for potatoes.

Jan had become a permanent fixture in our house by that time. He always arrived with something: a bit of sugar or flour for my mother, eggs for Arthur and me. Any ordinary need—a burlap sack to cover a broken window, a warm coat, aspirin for a fever, or medicine for my father's ulcer from Moizesevich (who supplied us even though it was forbidden to sell medicine to Jews)—became a calamity that necessitated devious machinations involving Jan in some way.

One night Suza's husband Munio had severe stomach pains and thought his appendix was inflamed. Dr. Meir Steuerman, our family doctor, was away, and the other Jewish doctors were in hiding. We sent someone to call the one Ukrainian doctor in town, a woman, but she refused to come because Munio was a Jew.

Jan volunteered to go to Borszczow for a doctor. He brought a Jewish doctor he knew there—the best one—in a horse and carriage to our Wasserman grandparents, where Munio and Suza were living. The doctor examined Munio, told him he did not have appendicitis but it was probably a blockage of the gut, and gave him something for the pain. Then Jan took the doctor back to Borszczow. All of us were stunned that he had done something like this for us. And he refused to accept any payment, not even to cover the hay for his horse.

One day a large quantity of "milk" was made available to Jews in a shop not far from our house. My mother pressed two jars into my arms and told me to run. On the way, I suddenly realized that I didn't have any money. Nonetheless I went on and joined the line, which was so long that I had little hope of getting even a few drops. "They call it milk," the man ahead of me said, "but it's only blue water left after the good milk is skimmed off." The woman behind me told him to get off the line, she'd be happy to take his portion.

I felt someone tugging at one of my jars. "Give them to me." It was Jan. This was where a cousin of his worked. He shifted the rifle to his other arm. Standing next to him, I suddenly felt his height, almost half again as tall as I was. And he was broad-shouldered. If I hadn't seen him around our house so much, hadn't seen my father brighten when he walked in the door and my mother stop her perpetual cleaning and sit down with him, I would have trembled, if not noticeably, then inside. Yet this man had a way of saying "Give them to me" that made it sound as if I were giving him a gift.

I told him that I had to fill one jar for my grandmother. He led me to the front of the line, gave me one full jar from the whitish liquid in the butter-churn machine, and told me to go home. The next day Grandmother Miriam reported that she had almost fainted when she saw a brute of a militiaman walking up to her door. He gave her the full jar and touched his cap. Imagine, he touched his cap to an old Jewish woman!

About a month or so later, Shimek and I were sharing the garden bench on a day of occasional soft breezes which made me impatient for spring to break through. I had lost my concentration for reading, but he immersed himself with more fervor than ever in the few books he could find.

He dropped a biography of Da Vinci from his lap as he tried to hold my hand. His hands were long, nicely shaped, and looked as if they didn't belong on his knobby, reddened wrists. He settled for linking pinkies with me. I looked straight ahead because if I turned my face to him, he might think I'd let him kiss me. We swung our pinkie-linked hands and then Shimek dropped the book again.

"Who *is* that guy?" Shimek looked toward the kitchen window, where my father was sitting with Jan and lighting his cigarette. I had been watching their little mime: Jan offered my father a cigarette, forgetting he didn't smoke, and my father, to show he didn't oppose smoking in others, struck a match while Jan put the tobacco pouch and papers in his pocket. The smoke came billowing out like a tattered handkerchief, the kind I ball up after a good cry and then smooth out again.

I told Shimek about Jan—that he came often, that he had bought things from us but mostly did us favors. Shimek said that a Ukrainian gave nothing for nothing, and that this one, never without his rifle, wore the no-nonsense expression of a policeman. "He's probably putting it on the bill," he said.

Chapter Twenty-one

GIRLS WERE ORDERED to work as maids for the Germans. For a bribe of three gold ducats, my father had arranged a compromise with the *Judenrat*: I would work for an officer in a capacity that would permit me to live at home. Since I had a knack for knitting, I became the personal sweater manufacturer for the Nazi chief manager of the count's estate, a swarthy *Volksdeutscher* (a member of the German ethnic minority in Poland), not at all an "Aryan" type.

Pepa, a school friend of mine, had the job of being his full-time mistress. She told me of his habit of carrying a whip in his right hand—and he enjoyed using it, she said. She told me, too, of the night-time "fun and games" at estate parties to which the *Judenrat* was forced to deliver beautiful women from the finest families. The cacophony of songs and breaking glass and screams was topped by target practice on champagne bottles. "Full ones," Pepa added. Sometimes you could hear the shots from their rifles in the middle of town.

Turtlenecks were the only style of sweater he fancied, and he paired them with riding breeches. Boots were very important for all the Germans, and they were constantly demanding them from the *Judenrat*, which got the leather from merchants who had hidden it to use as bribes to exempt their sons from forced servitude in labor camps. The *Judenrat* had Jewish shoemakers produce boots in various colors, black or brown, according to the Germans' whims. The *Judenrat* also supplied me with wool, also hidden by merchants, which I picked up at its headquarters. After I knitted the sweater sections at home, I had to go to the estate for fittings.

As I approached the gates of the estate, I talked sharply to myself: "Listen, he's a lowlife, a vain bully," but this didn't work very well. My hand trembled as I placed the package with the sweater sections on the table.

Without a word, the man stripped to the waist and stood stiffly in front of me in his black patent-leather boots. Since he was very tall, I had to stand on a stool to pin the front and back sections together. I could hear his breath accelerating, but he held back while I worked. In the pidgin Polish of a *Volksdeutscher*, he asked what colors of wool the *Judenrat* had on hand. "This off-white goes well with tan jodhpurs, don't you think?"

I assured him it did by polite-sounding grunts, since my mouth was full of pins.

The next one he wanted done in a modified cable stitch. "I bet you're good at more than knitting." His hand passed over my breasts.

I backed away and began folding up my knitting. "It will be ready the day after tomorrow." If I worked all day and half the night, I would have the sleeves knit, and the entire sweater sewn, ironed, and ready by then.

"Don't leave so quickly," he said. He pressed me to him, his hands spread on my buttocks.

I pushed him away. One powerful arm secured me to him again as he reached under my dress to touch me. The scent of his eau de cologne confused me. I began to cry.

He steered me to the bed. "The next thing you're going to tell me is you're a virgin." Anchoring me down with one arm, he allowed his free hand to roam under my dress.

"I am." I wanted to distract him but could hardly get any words out.

I felt the sharp tear of his nails as he reached under my panties with jabbing fingers.

"Unpin your hair and shake it out."

Undoing my hair brought me to a sitting position. I carefully placed each hairpin in a pile on my lap. Tears fell on my hands. "I am," I said again. "Is that so strange?"

"Not if you were my sister." As his two hands were wedging my knees apart, the hairpins rattled to the floor. A sob shook me. I fell on my knees and begged him to release me.

"Go," he said with a two-arm thrust, "your runny nose is ugly, and don't forget to deliver by noon on Thursday."

The next day, a peasant came to our house in a horsedrawn wagon with a big sack of potatoes from the *Volksdeutscher*, enough for us to live on for a few days. My parents didn't believe that he had given them to me without taking something in return, and people in town began talking.

Every time after that when I had to go to the estate I was terribly frightened. I kept telling myself that at worst, if I rebuffed him too much or too often, I would land in Czortkow prison—and my father would somehow find the money for a bribe for my release. Or I might be sent to a labor camp—and Jan would find a way to spring me from the train.

But going over these thoughts in my mind again and again as I walked to the estate could not calm my fears. One day, on my way over, a pain shot through my left armpit as if twine was being yanked through it, and the residual ache was intensified by a gnawing in my stomach not unlike hunger, yet different. Telling myself it was only fear didn't help. The physical pain remained. I talked to myself: Maybe this time he won't touch me. Sometimes my hands trembled so much when I was pinning the sweater sections on him that I couldn't put the pins in straight. Luckily, he never touched me again.

Chapter Twenty-two

J AN BROUGHT US news about what was happening, rumors about what was to come, and, of greatest importance, advance word of forced-labor roundups. What he didn't tell me until much later was how much his fellow militiamen resented the "important business" which he used as an excuse to get out of joining in the roundups so that he could warn us and be with us. They all knew about his relationship with me. "Are you something better?" they'd ask him. And a good friend of his had told him point-blank: "A Jewish girl isn't worth it." But they didn't report him. Maybe they were afraid of him, or maybe he had something on them.

That February, slave labor was demanded for the Borki-Wielki camp near Tarnopol, and no one showed up: by this time everyone knew what awaited them there. The Ukrainian militia picked men off the street and searched people's homes until the quota was filled. One of the men they picked up was my father. For some reason Jan could not help him get away and a bribe to the militia didn't work.

Packed in a train under armed guard, my father managed to escape in transit. When he came back home late the next night, he looked broken, as if he had long suffered under the whip. A further edict for additional slave laborers was issued. My father remained free by constantly sleeping at different relatives' houses, returning home on chance visits but rarely staying the night.

In April, on the first day of Passover, all men between the ages of twelve and sixty were ordered to go to Borszczow to be sent off to the Borki-Wielki labor camp. My father, Uncle Wolf, and Lolla's husband, Mottel, were among them. (Zygmunt didn't have to go because he was in the *Ordnungsdienst*.)

Skala was plunged into gloom. Only women, older people, children, and the sick were left in town, and they were consumed with worry about what was going to happen to the men. Uncle Zygmunt's sister, Serka, ran all the way to Borszczow to find out, and upon her return she reported that the men were being held at a concentration point where a selection was going to be made. Some would be working as shoemakers, carpenters, and at other skilled work, but many would be sent to the stone quarries and the slave-labor camps.

My father had noticed that if you claimed you had a profession you ended up at the stone quarry or performing hard labor on the count's estates, so he claimed to be an egg-packer employed in the warehouse on Grandfather Jakob's property, where eggs were preserved and packed for export to the Reich, a top-priority occupation. He pushed Uncle Wolf and Uncle Mottel to say that they, too, were egg-packers.

But after this, when the group he was held with was still waiting to find out what would be done with them, my father, Mottel, and Wolf managed to escape, and came running home at night, and they reported what had happened in Borszczow.

Some of the other men who had escaped were captured and sent to the Gestapo prison in Czortkow. Reports seeped out from the prison of brutal SS beatings of men forced to work until they dropped, of barbarities such as dogs sicced at their faces, and of whip-wielding torturers stomping prisoners to death with their boots. A prisoner friend of my father's who was redeemed by an enormous bribe told us of 120 Russian POW's forced to walk in a circle for ten hours a day with their hands in the air. It only took a few weeks before they were all dead.

We began to hear rumors that children, the sick, and old people would soon be "taken" in a full-scale raid. But "taken" where? and to do what? Children and the old and sick couldn't work on farms or in quarries or factories. Where would they be "taken"?

The children had no school to attend and nothing to do. I had tried to sit down at the kitchen table with Arthur and Aunt Lolla's boys and Uncle Wolf's daughters to go over with them the little bit of writing and arithmetic they'd learned and were fast forgetting, but visitors or chores had always interrupted us. I decided to start a school for Arthur, my cousins, and about six or seven other children, and proposed the idea to Shimek. Looking at the curtains hanging on the line in the corner of the yard, at their lace panels which would require slow hours of ironing before I could try to sell them, I decided to free up time for teaching by doing chores in the morning before everyone got up.

The children, who were seven and eight years old, came to my house, and Shimek and I shared with them as much knowledge as we could—a little reading, a little writing, some arithmetic. Sometimes Shimek brought an old book to read to them. We adjourned for the day when the children got too hungry to concentrate or when their mothers heard of rumors of a roundup and fearfully came to pick them up.

Arthur wasn't happy to have other kids around to spoil his solitary play, but he liked to do sums and liked even more to wipe the chalk from the small slate we used to demonstrate penmanship. It gave him a chance to lick the chalk dust on his fingers when his stomach growled, since we had no food to offer the children as snacks.

During the times our little school was in session, I enjoyed it hugely and thought I had a talent for dealing with children, and Shimek agreed. I encouraged them to tell me what was on their minds and spent afternoons with one or the other of them, interceding for one or another with a once-friend-turned-enemy or just holding him or her on my lap and singing. "You remind me of a St. Bernard," Shimek said to me.

On mornings when it was too cold or after an alarm that the

Germans were about to round up Jews, no children came, and it was just as well. Those mornings I didn't want to do anything except go to my little hiding place in the far corner of the yard where my father kept bits and pieces of lumber and lie there as if it were a life raft. The idea had come to me from a book I'd read about a person forced to abandon ship and float on a little boat on the wide, wide water. I didn't know how to swim, but on my raft I glided on waves under an open sky, oblivious to my mother's call. This kept me from drowning in the sea of rumor around me.

Hiding like a child coexisted with the other me who drove a hard bargain the next day to procure a whole box of candles for our lace curtains. Skala, the house, and the yard represented my childhood, and I wasn't ready to have it end.

Chapter Twenty-three

WITH RANDOM ROUNDUPS of Jews ever more frequent, it was becoming increasingly dangerous to venture out into the street, but now I faced an additional hazard. Gottschalk, a noncom in the Wehrmacht in his late twenties with a fleshy face, had a thing for me.

I could feel someone watching me even before he hovered behind or beside me, swathed in a huge black rain cape, or darted out in front of me and gripped my arm hard. "Those Mongol eyes, where did you get those Mongol eyes?" he would say, or, "We must have a rendezvous, you and I." He wagged his head close to my face, and his brandy breath invaded my nostrils. Gottschalk blocked my way, and I didn't dare move until he had enough of staring at me. One time, grinning gleefully, he jostled me so that the beets I had gathered rolled down the gutter, and he stood over me as I scrambled to pick them up. He knew I spoke German and tried to pry some minimal response out of me. "*Guten Morgen, Herr Feldwebel*" was all I allowed him.

Fear of being caught consorting with a member of a "polluted race" kept Gottschalk in check except on rainy nights, when he would come to the house to look for me. On those nights, I slept in Uncle Wolfe's villa at the end of the lumber yard.

One rainy night, he and another soldier arrived at our door, pistols in hand. I wasn't home. He put his gun against my mother's head and demanded, "Where's your daughter?"

"I don't know," she replied and told them to search the house if they didn't believe her. His pal slapped her, threw her against the stove, and beat her with the broom handle while Gottschalk stood there egging him on.

"He's from Vienna, a backwater town. Beating is second nature for him," Gottschalk said. "I'm from Berlin." My mother repeated this remark several times during the four weeks she spent in bed recovering from the beating. "From Berlin," she said, "a superior type from Berlin."

Unable to find me, Gottschalk and his henchman left and went looking for me at the home of one of my aunts. When they didn't find me there, they raped her and forced her husband to watch. The rape had to be kept secret because if the Gestapo found out about it they would have killed her immediately, since Germans were forbidden to "fraternize" with "subhuman" Jews. My aunt told a few members of the family but they didn't believe her—they didn't want to hear or know about it. She never told her children, and for that reason, I have not disclosed her name.

Lotka's parents had a hiding place in their cellar. The Sternbergs had returned from Lvov, where they had been living during the Russian occupation, when the Germans invaded eastern Poland. (My father's brother Leo and his family did the same thing.) Perhaps they thought it would be easier to get food from the peasants in the Skala area.

The Sternbergs' hideout was a crawl space meant for a few hours' sanctuary—a narrow passage behind a false stone wall. The entrance was a hole in the wall concealed by shelves with jars on them.

For the next two nights after the rape, Lotka and I slept in this hiding place. I should say spent the night, not slept, because it was impossible to lie down, and we were too nervous to fall asleep anyway.

For air we had the wintry drafts that hit that side of the house. We lay scrunched on a blanket, my head resting on the pillow of her feet until we switched places. We ate boiled turnips and bread. Actually, it was a sort of feast, since my mother had smeared some goose grease on the bread. We told each other stories as we ate, and laughed out of shared anxiety. Then we heard a clomp, clomp from above: a signal to remain quiet. What was the use of hiding, the clomp said, if you're going to giggle and give yourselves away?

Chapter Twenty-four

ONE NIGHT, when there was a rumor of a raid, Jan brought me to his home to spend the night in his room. When his mother saw that he had brought in a girl who was not his fiancée, and one so obviously Jewish-looking, she ran out of the house. His sister and her husband also saw me; they didn't say a word. Jan could see how upset they were.

His room was immaculately clean, and his bed had pillows and an embroidered comforter. I lay on the bed, terribly frightened. Jan sat by my side all night, watching me like a faithful dog. Very early the next morning, he gave me a jar of honey and sent me home.

Later that afternoon, Jan came to the house to make sure I'd arrived home safely. As we stood in the entrance hall, he said he had made a decision. He had broken his engagement to his blond fiancée. He was not going to marry her, he said. The engagement and the marriage date had already been officially announced in church, and his ex-fiancée's father had let it be known that he'd avenge the insult.

Taking my hand, he told me that he loved me, and that he would do anything to save my life, to make sure that they wouldn't get me, that he'd grab me away from the *Umschlagplatz* or pull me off the train; wherever I was during an *aktsia* he'd get to me and not let them take me away, even if he had to murder someone. Then he kissed me lightly—the first time he had done so.

Jan's declaration of love came as a surprise—totally unexpected. But it made me calm, gave me a sense of protection, acting as a kind of shield around me as I navigated in an increasingly hostile and stormy sea.

In June, the order came down for seventy-five girls to be sent to a labor camp, but only six reported. News of a night raid instigated by Hera filtered down to Jan, and he came to get me—this time waiting until his mother, sister, and brother-in-law were already asleep.

This was the first time he brought me to the hiding place behind the false wall he had built in the hayloft of his barn. The sloping roof was so low that I hit my head as I made my way to the "bed," a pile of hay. He warned me that I was not to make a sound if he saw anyone in the yard, and told me there was a chamber pot in the corner if I needed it.

Jan moved a bale of hay adjacent to the triangular window opening, sat down on it, and lit a cigarette.

I lay down but heard my heart beat so loudly that I sat up.

"Don't be afraid," he said. "No one will hurt you tonight." I asked him what was going to happen.

"They're taking the girls to the work camp near Jagelnica. Single ones only." He paused, then smiled. "Will that make you leap into marriage?"

We laughed, each for different reasons, and he pulled a hunk of bread out of his pocket for me. "Watch the crumbs—mice, you know."

When Jan knew for certain that the transport of girls had left, he told me I could go home. I saw that each Jewish house had a Star of David either painted on its wall or hung in the window. My parents had feared I had been caught in the roundup. For a minute each stood alone as I entered, then in a rush they came toward me together. I asked my father why we didn't have a

Jewish star displayed, and he said, "Jan will tell us when to hang it out."

Barely credible stories began to float around, stories told by distraught escapees from different *shtetls* and by malicious peasants about Jews forced to dig their own graves before they were shot.

My father, who had come to realize that the Germans in Skala were not the Germans of the poetry he knew by heart, began to prepare hiding places for the family, not only the four of us, but my grandparents, aunts, uncles, and cousins as well. Jan procured materials for building the hideouts, and my father showed him their location.

All the hiding places were on Grandfather Jakob's property. My father built no hideouts at our house, wisely fearing that the Ukrainians would come to look for him there and then would find the rest of us, too. The first hideout he built was under the tub in my grandmother's bathhouse, which had an earth floor. There was a camouflaged square cutout which could be pulled up to allow us to descend into the hole via a tiny stepladder.

We had a few practice sessions at night to see how quickly we could learn to hide in it, and though Arthur had to be woken up, he wasn't cranky. He thought of it as a spy adventure, or perhaps he welcomed the change of expression on my parents' faces, since afterwards, when we sat in the kitchen drinking ersatz tea, the furrows between my father's eyes eased and my mother's hands, for a change, lay folded in her lap. By August, when all houses had to be marked with a Jewish star, we were spending our nights—sleeplessly—in this hole in the ground.

Meanwhile, my father began the backbreaking labor of building the larger hideout under the floor of the egg warehouse with the help of my uncles. This was the hiding place which was to save the lives of sixteen members of our family and two neighbors during the *aktsia*.

We had two rings left; except for my mother's heart pendant, all the rest of our jewelry had been bartered for provisions. I accompanied my father one day when he brought the diamond ring to Father Derewienko, who was now a kind of chaplain to the Ukrainian militia. The priest took the little leather pouch containing the ring and put it in a large cabinet in his living room.

My father told me, as we left the house, that the ring wouldn't bring much money, but it had been his mother, Hinda's, engagement ring, and we should try to keep it in the family. "Someday," he said, "it will be yours."

Chapter Twenty-five

MY MOTHER WAS on her hands and knees scrubbing the wooden floor to perfect whiteness. It was Friday, the day of the week she worked the hardest, and since cooking and baking was no longer time-consuming, she prepared for the Sabbath by giving an extra scrubbing to the center hall, which usually lay protected by a two-layered rug plus newspaper when it rained.

My father burst into the house. "You crazy woman," he said, kicking over the pail so that water sloshed halfway up the wall. The shock of my father's violent act drove me to strike him, but before my punch reached his chest he grabbed me, held me, and I fought free. My mother sat on the floor, legs spread, rag held high, her arm gyrating in the air as if she were wiping a window to see out through the grime.

A blast of smoke rushed at me through the open front door. I looked across the street and saw the reason for the anguish on my father's face: the large synagogue was burning! Jews were running in and out, trying desperately to save the burning Torah scrolls.

I dashed out of the house to the synagogue. Jews who had gathered there told me that ten old men were being held hostage under guard in the marketplace square. Two could be my grand-fathers. I had to go there. The ten elderly men—all highly respected but not my grandfathers—were shoved and slapped, kicked and pulled by their beards and hair. They maintained a concerted silence while the Ukrainian militia stepped up the pace of their assault. Someone came up close behind me. "Go home." Jan's voice came through as more of a plea than an order. I left without turning around.

Later, my father told me that the hostages had been released. They and other Jews put on their prayer-shawls, fasted and prayed, and then took the burnt Torah scrolls they had pulled out of the flames down the hill to the Jewish cemetery, where they buried them.

My father got a letter from his sister Esther in Nazi-occupied Paris. She wrote that the Germans were demanding that Jews with Polish citizenship register at the prefecture to be sent back to Poland. Aunt Esther asked him if it would be better for them to come home rather than risk hiding in France. Would they be safe, she asked.

My father wrote Esther a postcard with one sentence: "When you come home, you will probably first see your mother." Since Grandmother Hinda had died during the Soviet regime, this meant they would be going to their deaths.

The postcard, which was miraculously delivered, saved the lives of my aunts, uncles, and cousins in Paris, they told me after the war. Instead of reporting for deportation to Poland, they fled to Vichy, and later went into hiding when the Germans took over "unoccupied" France. They all survived.

Erev Succos, September 25, 1942. Kelner, the SS commander of the region, came to Skala from the Gestapo headquarters in Czortkow, demanding from the *Judenrat* "gifts" of leather and gold pieces in return for letting the Jews remain in town.

Just before noon he, a few soldiers, and several members of the *Judenrat* burst through the door to our house. Without a glance at my mother, Arthur, and me—my father wasn't at home—Kelner ordered the soldiers to check each room, including the attic, for furniture and other valuables. Since anything of value had already been taken, there wasn't much for his deputy to record in his notebook.

Kelner conducted a little search himself under the bed, in the cupboards, and through the closets. "You," he said to my mother, addressing her politely in the second-person plural, "you have lived in Germany?" My mother barely managed to shake her head. "Remarkable," he said to one of his soldiers, "but under her petticoat she's as filthy as all the other dirty sows."

Kelner left a message for my absent father: if he did not appear at headquarters by the end of the day, we would all be shot.

Later in the afternoon, it looked like we might have a decent *Succos*. Kelner, seemingly pleased with his loot, had announced, "The Jews of Skala have nothing to fear."

When my father came home from the hiding place he had spent the night in with Uncle Wolf, he was relieved that we hadn't been harmed. But he didn't believe Kelner and had a feeling that something was brewing. "They'll come for us when we least expect it," he said. He insisted we all go immediately to the hiding place in the bathhouse and spend the night there.

Arthur and I begged him to relent, to excuse us from heading right away to the hiding place in the bowels of the earth. We wanted to join the rest of the family for dinner at my Wasserman grandparents' house, as we always did on the eve of Jewish holidays. If there was an alarm, we argued, we could all rush to the larger hiding place in the warehouse that my father and uncles had just finished building. My father reluctantly agreed. "It's far from the house," he said, "so run as fast as you can."

I was ready to risk my life to go to my grandparents for dinner. It was the eve of my eighteenth birthday, and all the relatives gathered around the table for the holiday would make it a celebration.

I had been tempted many times to barter my curlers away, and now I realized why I hadn't. The hairdo I would sport tomorrow would make me feel festive all day. And rolling my hair up in rows of metal coils and sleeping on them, despite the discomfort or maybe because of it, was my last vestige of dignity.

IV

Hiding After the *Aktsia* (September 1942– August 1943)

Chapter Twenty-six

"**D**O YOU HAVE any idea what you looked like when you stepped out of the hiding place with your hand full of curlers and your hair twisted into writhing black snakes?"

Jan and I had settled ourselves at the window of the attic hideout in his barn. Arthur was asleep, and Jan and I were keeping watch for the approach of soldiers, for the inevitable attack sure to happen in five minutes—or next week.

We tried to appear calm for each other, but once in a while Jan revealed his anxiety when he raised himself to his knees and angled his body at the sides of the window to get a view of anyone who might be skulking around the barn.

I told him that I hadn't been thinking of anything at the moment we emerged from the hideout except how glad I was to be alive and how good it was to hug him.

"Jan, tell me, what were you doing there?" He told me that he had been watching the warehouse the entire time we were hidden in the hole under its floor. Jan had been keeping a lookout on our house as well. The woman and child who had made us take them into our warehouse hideout were the aunt and cousin of a Jewish barber we knew slightly. They had come to stay with our neighbors, the family of a kosher butcher who were their cousins.

The barber's aunt had apparently told the barber about our hideout, because during the *aktsia* he left his bunker, found Jan, and tried to make a deal with him: he would reveal our whereabouts in return for the release of his mother, who had already been seized by the Germans and was being held at the *Umschlagplatz*. Eighteen for one, and Jan would get the "credit."

"He was going to tell the Germans where we were hiding, with his own aunt and cousin there, too?"

"Yes," replied Jan, "to save his mother. But I told him that I would kill him if he did it. I had to watch him, too, and make sure he didn't leave his own bunker again to go to the Germans."

Jan's face looked peaked with anger, his eyes wide and unblinking.

"Would you really have killed him?"

"Yes," he said.

In a half-crouch to protect his head from the sloping beams, which seemed at times to reach out like tentacle-holding hammers to clobber unsuspecting heads, he came over to put his arms around me. I had started to shiver from the chill that comes before dawn. Soothing me as if I were a child with a scraped knee, he kept assuring me that he would look after me and that with him I was safe. I remember seeing the dark patch inside the window frame turn light as we sat there, Jan holding me on his lap, his arms around me.

"You don't need curlers in your hair," he said. "It's beautiful as it is."

The sun's light in Jan's attic was almost as brilliant as the moon's had been by the time I settled into my cubby in the hay. I lay with my eyes open, reluctant to enter the twilight of sleep, the night behind my eyes from which there was no escape.

Chapter Twenty-seven

IN THE NEXT TWO WEEKS, Jan regularly came to see us about an hour after the house grew dark.

We'd hear him coming into the barn below our loft, and then there would be a short interval before he appeared at the top of the ladder. That was when he changed into the barn clothes he kept hidden behind the straw in order to keep his regular clothes free of hay and the odor of the barn. Before he left, he would change back into the good clothes he left near the barn door with his rifle. Jan also hid the ladder he used to climb up to our attic hiding place. It was a long and rickety ladder which he had made himself and which had to be pried apart and folded up.

Jan had obviously thought all this out very carefully. Working out his daily plan for taking care of us was a full-time job.

Every time Jan came, he'd bring us food—a piece of sausage or some apples or at least a hunk of bread, or a few raw eggs which we would eat with the bread if we had any. One time he brought a jar of delicious borscht, unlike any I'd ever tasted; he disposed of the jar far away from the house. Another time he came swinging the handle of a can of pork stew. It had gotten cold but it tasted delicious. I used my index finger to scrape out the last of the sauce, and so did Arthur.

Most of the food he brought us he stole from his mother, sometimes from her cooking pot and sometimes from his own portion. He had to hide it because his mother, as a typical peasant woman, knew exactly how much food she had on hand.

Jan's brother-in-law gave us a scare when he visited the barn one day, muttering while searching for the hidden ladder, and then giving up and cursing when he heard his wife call him. Some days later, Jan's sister was crossing the yard on her way to the little garden shed; as I watched through the crack between two planks of the barn wall, she looked up at the window, standing and studying it for a long while, and then continued on. Perhaps she had caught a glimpse of Arthur's head; occasionally he forgot that he was not permitted to go near the window.

I asked Jan to bring me the suitcase of clothes—beautiful suits from Paris and silk robes and dresses—that my mother had given him for safekeeping before she and my father went to the ghetto so I could give some of them to his sister. It was gone, he told me. His mother and sister must have found it.

Jan told me that his mother, experiencing chest pains, had summoned him to her bedside and told him that it would kill her if she learned that he was helping us. She had pressed her hand over her heart to remind Jan that she had already lost his father and asked if he wanted her to lose him too.

What could I say? If I took Arthur by the hand and started walking, where would I go? I had to think of Arthur's life as well as my own. If he was caught, he'd be shipped off to Belzec, and he was too young to join me in a fugitive existence. Yet if we stayed and were caught, Jan's life would be forfeited.

I begged Jan to take us somewhere else, and yet this hidden corner of a barn's attic was the only safe place in the world for me. Arrangements were being made, he said, and added, "Be good." I got angry at him and started to raise my voice. "We're going before it gets light." He slid next to me on the straw and clamped his hand over my mouth. The firm pressure of his fingers on my lips pressed my frustration down but not out.

"Until I find a place, you stay here," Jan said.

I decided to chance it a few more days. For Arthur, I told

myself. Jan rocked me back and forth in his arms and we did a sort of melded hop on our buttocks, I holding him at the waist as I abandoned myself to the swing of our bodies. Arthur woke with a whimper and Jan gave him a piece of bread. Then he disappeared down the ladder and I continued the hop solo.

Chapter Twenty-eight

I LONGED FOR word from my parents. Jan could tell me nothing more than that he'd heard they were safe and that they had a hard life in the Borszczow ghetto.

One day he brought the news that our house had been taken over by the Germans for offices, since it had the reputation of being the cleanest one in Skala. This made me burst into a high, ironic laugh, and Jan had to cover my mouth to blunt the sound of its maniacal edge.

The days were rolled into a tight coil of waiting—waiting for Jan to bring more news of my parents or something to eat or just to come and sit with me while Arthur slept. Most of all I waited for the moment of discovery, for the Gestapo and Ukrainian militia to pounce and kick out. Even though Jan had assured me he would spring me from any truck or train they shoved me into, I knew the odds favored their killing us right in front of the barn.

I had a yen to write letters, to tell someone—Churchill or Stalin—to hurry up and end the war, but didn't ask Jan to bring paper for letters or a diary; he had enough trouble scrounging for food without looking for writing materials. And the murk of the hayloft made writing or reading impossible, which was just as well, since there was nothing to read anyway.

Time, plentiful time, added an ineffable peril to the real fears. "True time," during which I sat and stared at a clump of hay and followed my thoughts as they slipped wherever they wished, clashed with "false time," chronological time, during which I gave my attention to Arthur or Jan. How to orient myself from one variety of time to the other without feeling violently unsettled became the task of waiting.

Arthur seemed to be better at existing in limbo than I. He fell into long periods of sleep, and I often hobbled over to him on my knees to check if he was still breathing. During sessions of "true time," when my body hung suspended over the straw-covered floor, my mind jumped about to ingenious schemes, to ways I could distract the attackers so Arthur could flee.

Chronological time had become meaningless, since I had no clock or watch. On gray days, time played tricks: I'd think it must be eight o'clock in the morning and it would turn out to be five. The neighbor's rooster could be counted on some of the time, but then one day his crowing stopped. Had he been sold or eaten by his owners? I made up stories for Arthur about the fate of the rooster. The saga began to fascinate me as well as him. I named the rooster Phoenix. "Tell me another Phoenix," he said several times a day.

I trained myself to become more and more adept at using "false time" to advantage. Sometimes I managed to get Arthur to join me in braiding straw figures. I made a whole settlement of houses and people for him to play with. Other times I made up new stanzas for old songs, and Arthur joined in the refrain.

Arthur preferred to hear wish-dreams of what we would eat when the war was over, so I served up imaginary platters of meat and potatoes. His stomach had not shrunken. One day we had a piece of bread and I gave Arthur part of my share. I prayed he wouldn't eat it all, but he did. How can I be so mean, I accused myself, to wish the food in Arthur's mouth into mine? My stomach rarely growled; instead, a continual sensation of hollow-

ness reminded me of a yawning vase fated to sit on a table
without flower or water.

Losing track of the days led to chunks of them being outside of
calendar time, but the November chill clearly made itself felt.
"Bitter weather," the conventional term we used for extreme
cold, gained new meaning. As a child, when I heard my mother
say, "It's bitter outside," I saw wrinkled almonds hanging in
frosty air. Now "bitter" came in the form of the shivers, in
watching my breath solidify as I sat in a coat of straw. Jan came
with rags to stuff between the wall planks, but there wasn't
much he could do about the window-hole. He hung a double
sack as a curtain.

Sitting on my legs kept them warm, but I had to remember to
shake the cramp out once in a while. I realized how fortunate
we'd been while still living in our own house: I could stand
without stooping and could go out to look for bread.

Day by day my legs began to atrophy, the deadening assuaged
only when Jan came to give Arthur and me a late-night chance
once a week to trot around the barn floor. Usually Arthur was
too sleepy. Up in the hayloft again, I sat as inert as a pitchfork
sticking out of a bale of hay. My unused legs cried to dance.
Dancing with a partner—a smooth fox-trot with numerous
dips—became my favorite fantasy, but my partner's face remained obscured. A few times it was my father's.

Once, when Jan took me down the ladder to let me exercise
my legs, he caught me in a bear hug and whirled me around,
and I let myself go limp, enjoying the vertigo until he finally
steadied me back onto my feet. It spoiled it to remain absolutely
silent, to force myself to swallow even a small laugh.

The smell of Jan's skin as my nose grazed his neck entered my
mouth and became an agreeable taste, like a juicy pear or apple.
When we sat or stood near each other I found the mix of damp
wool from his jacket combined with the odor of male skin fresh
from the outdoors an intoxicant, a kind of magnetic ingredient.
At times I felt heat flash for a moment across my forearms and
chest and burn in my cheeks.

Sometimes when Jan held my hand loosely while we sat together at the little window, he pressed it slightly, just a layer of gauze over palm and fingers, and I'd find myself hoping he'd do it more and harder.

Chapter Twenty-nine

DURING THE LONG NIGHTS in the attic, Jan and I told each other about our lives, what we'd done and what we expected to do. We excluded present time, the war, its ferocity, its irrationality; the hours spent in the attic seemed borrowed, not real, because they were unbidden.

What an unlikely pair we made: a Ukrainian shoemaker and a Jewish high school girl! We had begun to think of ourselves as a couple, each one finding in the other someone to confide in, a person with whom to share an impermissible yearning or a strange dream.

I told him uncensored stories in the belief that if I didn't offer them now, no one might ever hear them. I told him about cheating on the oral exams with the Russian teachers. Jan admitted to poaching a goose at age eleven and told me some tales of early love-making which involved a lot of hay, moonlight, and lost undergarments. I told him about Izio.

"So you like older men," Jan said.

"Not necessarily," I said. "I like Shimek. But boys my own age are so childish."

He told me that his ex-fiancée had married someone on the rebound, and that her father had it in for him, and had called him a "Jewish uncle" right to his face. He didn't care, let people say what they like. But Dzsisiak, Jan said, had better not talk like that to the Germans or it would cost him his life.

"Aren't you going to get married?" I asked.

"I have my eye on someone, but I'm not in a hurry. And you, you must become a doctor," he said, as if he were sure that the war's end would find me still alive. "Why not study in Warsaw? I'd like to see Warsaw, but Paris is out. I can't speak French."

"I'll teach you," I said, and he broke into a broad grin, saying he'd hold me to it. I began right then with "*Bonjour*," and he said it in such a funny way that I couldn't help laughing, and he began to laugh, too, while repeating the word. In a final burst of frustrated energy, he put his arms around me and pressed his lips on my cheek. Somehow, in the instant between bubbles of laughter, we stopped, and he kissed me on the lips, a light friendly kiss, and I thought of giving one back, but it was too late. He was back at his post at the window.

When we were alone without immediate threat, when we talked or sat silently, we had a way of looking into each other's eyes that was not embarrassing—a kind of state of undress in which I felt no hint of nakedness. Several times he was at the point of giving me more than a casual kiss, but the moment never seemed to be right.

One morning I bunched my handkerchief under the apple Jan had brought so that it made a fluffy doily, the white cambric setting off the tawny orange and yellow-green of the apple skin, which I had polished to a high gloss. When Arthur woke I would cut a third of it for our breakfast and save the sharp-edged core for myself. The seeds were chewy and perhaps had some healthful properties.

Riveted by the sheen of the apple, I let my thoughts wander to Sluwa Kassierer, our homework tutor. I remembered how one day when I was twelve, I had remained to finish a composition after the other pupils had left and saw Sluwa pick up an apple, wield it in the cup of her joined palms, then twirl it by its stem. "I've never tasted the apple from the forbidden tree," she said, and there was great yearning in her voice and eyes.

I had wondered at the time what she meant but had not dared ask, and now I knew she had been longing for a man's embrace. But tasting that "apple" was forbidden her as an unmarried woman.

I remembered how, when I was a high school student a few years later, I read *Nana* and associated the prospect of sexual pleasure with a boudoir and its fragrance of sultry blooms, the room a pink shrine for a soft bed from which ecstatic sighs of love-making rose at intervals. Now I lay on a pallet of straw. And whom did I see next to me in my mind's eye? I glimpsed a tall figure, the head turned away. Sore-boned and itchy, picking bugs off my clothes and spitting one out of my mouth, I realized how little I resembled that foolish young girl.

Taste of the forbidden apple. The shiny cheeks of the apple on its doily taunted me to take a bite.

Arthur slept and woke and ate his apple section and played a secret game in a straw fort he made with his jacket in the corner. The cold days of autumn turned his hands blue before he stopped, lay down on his back, and, crossing his arms, bedded his rigid hands under his armpits.

Looking at him, I realized how dangerous it was to fall so deeply into reverie. I was living so actively in a dream world that it was hard for me to rev up my fear mechanism again. I was responsible for Arthur. I vowed to train myself out of daydreaming.

Chapter Thirty

AFTER TWO WEEKS in Jan's attic hideout, my dreams began to shift from plates of schnitzel with eggs and anchovies and bowls of cherries with cream to waterfalls, rivers, rain. Not thirst but dirt—the feel of oily skin chafing under unwashed underclothes—bothered me constantly.

Jan brought us enough water to drink and to rinse our hands, but warm water and soap were luxuries of the past. Not washing didn't trouble Arthur, and when I tried to comb my fingers through his hair to untangle it, he pulled away. I didn't know if the rank odor I smelled came from me or the barn. Arthur said it was me. That night I told Jan to forget about food the next day and arrange an ersatz bath for us.

The next Sunday, when his family had left home to go to church and Arthur had been asleep for a long time, Jan appeared at the top of the ladder and led me down to the barn. He handed me a pail of hot water, a hunk of brown soap, and a piece of torn cloth, and apologized for not bringing a better towel.

In my eagerness to catch the fading heat of the water, I rolled down my stockings while Jan unbuttoned my sweater. I shyly turned my back as he gently soaped the nape of my neck. My undershirt became soaked, and I tore it and my bra and panties off, too.

It seemed natural to stand there on the straw-covered planks and have Jan scrub my legs and arms and then hand me the soap so I could do the rest. He told me to kneel and hold my head back and he poured water over my hair, then worked some soap into it.

Finally he dumped the entire pail of water over me, and I said, "But what about Arthur?" He promised to bring some more hot water another day. Then he produced a clean shirt, a boy's shirt of coarse weave but with the odor of sun-drying, and I wrapped it around myself like a sheepskin coat. We returned to the attic and, seated by the window as usual, Jan signaled with his head for me to come, and I sat in the niche of his legs below his knees, feeling light and new. He kissed my wet hair and I fell asleep.

It seems odd to me now that such a simple procedure as a makeshift bath could switch my mood from low to high or, to put it more accurately, from a state of terror of imminent, violent death to a feeling of calm bordering on joy and even hope that this nightmare would end.

That it would end, that I would survive, was still my gut conviction. My father had said I would go to Paris and study medicine. I held on to that plan. It had become a mantra: Paris, Paris, Paris. The pictures that flashed across my mind were a succession of images: the Eiffel Tower, my father's books by Dumas, my Aunt Esther's face on an old photograph, a loaf of the long, onion-colored tube of white bread she had brought us on one of her visits to Skala.

One night when Jan didn't come by, I heard the barn door's hinges creak and some voices whispering below. My first thought was to wake Arthur. The sounds were soft—perhaps a nosy neighbor or Jan's brother-in-law coming to get something in the barn. Maybe some people in flight looking for shelter. I held my breath and pressed my ear to a crack between the floorboards.

I heard a familiar clearing of the throat. No mistake, it was my father. And yes, of course, the other voice was my mother's.

Tossing the straw away, I stuck my head down through the attic opening. "We're here," they whispered.

No ladder. I didn't know where it was hidden, and they couldn't find it.

It wasn't until the following night, when Jan came by, that they were able to climb up to the attic, and Arthur and I hugged their shoulders before they reached the top rung and could step out onto the floor. The four of us and Jan were together again! My father looked paler than ever, and I had forgotten how my mother had thinned out during the past year. She kept shaking her head from right to left in a continual "no," as if she couldn't believe she was seeing her children again. Sitting on the loft floor, she looked up at Arthur standing in front of her and said he looked taller, but her head moved to deny it.

My father told us about the Borszczow ghetto, a few streets in what had once been the poorest neighborhood, with run-down buildings and no sewers. It didn't take a genius to figure out that the Germans had massed the Jews together because it would be easier to dispose of them that way. "Living there we were already dead," he said. There was almost no food or fuel for the communal stove in the room he and my mother shared with eleven other Jews.

My father knew one of the leaders of the *Judenrat*. Weeks of bribing and wheedling—begging for his life—had finally loosened a link in the *Judenrat* chain, allowing him and my mother to escape. They had run the 15 kilometers from Borszczow to Jan's barn, and miracle of miracles: they were here.

My father and Jan talked a long time, examining all our alternatives. None of the hiding places my father had built were safe, and escaping to the forest, where the fascist "partisans" were killing Jews, was worse than staying in the ghetto. It was decided that they would stay here until Jan could work something out with people he knew in a distant village.

Jan took two apples and a penknife out of his pocket and cut each one in half. After he disappeared down the ladder, I watched him hide the knife in a false closet he'd made in the wall. The sharp slope of the roof—which even on its high end prevented all of us except Arthur from standing up straight—

gave my parents the slant of cripples as they moved to the hay bed. They fell asleep the instant they lay down.

In the moments before sleep, when I had the warmth of my father and mother on both sides of me, I marveled at how swiftly the time had passed; a large block of "false time" had canceled the "true" kind for a change, and I was happy.

Chapter Thirty-one

WE KNEW WE COULDN'T all stay in Jan's barn hideout indefinitely and racked our brains for possible permanent hiding places. My father dispatched Jan to bring Marysia, the peasant woman from a nearby village who had worked for us after Arthur was born. At that time, she had just given birth to a child out of wedlock whom she had to leave in the village. In our house she had a tiny alcove for a room and had worked night and day. The family had laughed at her way of repositioning cleaned rugs on the floor with a ruler, but no one could deny that when they were hanging on the line, she beat them harder and longer than any other servant had ever done.

But Marysia refused to come. Then one night after midnight, when Jan had stopped in to bring us a can of milk and empty our waste pail, we heard little taps on the barn door. Jan sprang toward the ladder with an agility that I would not have imagined in a man with such a large, tightly molded body had I not then seen—through a chink in the attic floor—how it served him in taking leaps to the door. Arthur must have been sleeping lightly, because he sat up in his hay bed and hugged his jacket, which doubled as a blanket.

When Marysia reached the top of the ladder, she barely

acknowledged us and headed straight for Arthur. He seemed glad to see her, too. She pinched his cheek and handed him a sweet roll wrapped in a cloth. When he finished eating, she blew her nose in the cloth and put it in her pocket.

She explained to Jan why it had taken so many days for her to get here: she was being watched—and so was he. He should be more careful; it had been foolish to come to see her during the daylight. Neighbors would wonder why a poor woman who had no money to buy looted material would have a visitor, especially one connected to her former employers. Everyone knew that Jan was Benjamin Gottesfeld's "Jewish uncle" and that the family had not been caught. It wouldn't be long, Marysia warned, before they found us.

After Marysia refused my father's offer of money to take Arthur and me, my mother moved toward her. She had forgotten how Marysia had been afraid of her, so afraid because of my mother's obsession with cleanliness that she had cleaned my father's razor and cut her hand. She bled for four weeks. My mother thought nothing of the fact that Marysia didn't share our meals or even the same food and usually just got the bread left over after we had finished eating—that was the way things were done.

She believed that she and Marysia had been on cordial mistress-servant terms in the past due to an occasional bonus of a discarded pair of shoes or a plate that was no longer useful. Marysia had always appeared pleased with the gifts, and at Christmas and Easter, she had brought us samples of holiday goodies from home, which, of course, we could not eat because they weren't kosher. Although my mother had not permitted her to nail her crucifix on the wall above her little bed in her alcove room, she closed an ear when Marysia told Arthur stories from the New Testament.

"You have no right to ask me to take Arthur," Marysia said as my mother bent to kiss her hand and fell to her knees.

"Why did you come, then?" I asked.

"I came to see Arthur . . ." I knew she had stopped herself from saying "for the last time" as she gently twisted a lock of his hair and traced the line of his cheeks to his chin.

"Be a brave boy," she said and turned to go down the ladder.

Arthur found his niche in the straw and began to suck his thumb, a habit he'd dropped long before.

My mother regretted that she hadn't given Marysia better things in the past: "Then she would have taken the children." My father assured her that it wouldn't have helped. By taking us, Marysia would be putting her life in danger, and she had the right to refuse, he said. In one of the neighboring villages, the houses of people who had been hiding Jews had been burned—a few with their owners still inside them. Jan personally knew a Polish family the Germans had shot when Jews were found hiding in their chicken coop.

The risk Marysia's visit put us in flew to the forefront of our minds. Even if she herself didn't report us to the authorities, she might carelessly allude to her visit during a neighborly chat and someone might then denounce us to the Gestapo. Before the *aktsia*, we had been reviled human beings living in precarious times but not in immediate mortal danger. Now, after the *aktsia*, we had become hunted creatures.

My parents decided to go back home. From there, my father could try to arrange a refuge for himself and my mother, and possibly even for Arthur and me. They had no choice: Jan could barely find enough food to keep two people alive. They also knew that each additional person, through some inadvertent like coughing or sneezing at the wrong moment, presented a hazard.

One night Jan led them out while Arthur and I were asleep.

Chapter Thirty-two

SEVERAL DAYS LATER, Jan brought us to the home of Lotka's parents, Mottel and Szencia Sternberg, where my parents were now living. Mottel, who spoke fluent German, had managed to get himself certified as a *Wertvolle Jude*, a Jew who worked for the Gestapo. He, Szencia, and Lotka had hidden during the *aktsia* and the three days before Mottel got a "hard" certificate—one that would stand up well under scrutiny—in the crawl-space where Lotka and I had spent the two nights after my aunt's rape. What Mottel did in working directly for a Gestapo chief no one knew.

"Like wild animals," my mother said as she drew Arthur and me over the doorstep of the Sternberg's house. It was true; we looked like wild animals. We were dirty—straw and vermin sticking to our clothes, our hair matted and snarled; and we smelled, I imagined, of rotted farm feed too long out of the sun.

She put an arm around each of us and then hugged Arthur and me separately. Then it was my father's turn. Tears edged down from my mother's eyes.

"Animals don't cry," said Arthur.

We went to our room in the back part of the house; the Sternbergs had the other room. Our high-ceiling room had a bed for my parents and a cot I was to share with Arthur, both pushed flush against opposite walls, a chest, two chairs, and a table made of a plank sitting on two barrels. The kitchen was closed off, and we did our cooking on the wood-burning stove in the back hall leading out to the garden. "Even the pot and plate belong to Mottel and Szencia," my mother said.

That first night, Arthur and I attacked the large plate of cold potatoes my mother set on the table with the ravenous gusto of starved beasts. For once I didn't say to myself, Please don't let Arthur eat so much. Whom had I entreated? God? Either He was deaf or dead or I didn't know His language.

My parents just sat silently and watched us.

They told me that Lotka was passing as a Christian in Lvov. The Polish priest who had given religious instruction to the Catholic children in the Polish elementary school before the war, and who had since then sheltered several Jews, had taught Lotka Catholic prayers and liturgy every night for four weeks. He had gotten her "good" Aryan papers—those of somebody who had died—and had made the arrangements for a middleman to take her to live with a Polish couple as their niece in return for money sent with him by Lotka's parents.

Almost beaming, my father then told us of our immense luck: he could walk the streets freely because he had a *W*, a big round metal badge pinned on to the lapel of his jacket, an insignia based on a certificate testifying that he was a *Wirschaftswichtige Jude*, a Jew essential to the economy. The essential service he was supposed to be performing was gathering scrap metal for conversion to ammunition for the war industry.

My father had bought the certificate and badge from a Ukrainian gangster—a thief, gambler, drunk, and womanizer who had grown up near Jews and spoke fluent Yiddish—with some of the silver he had buried in the yard. But the certificate was a "soft" one because the metal and rags he was supposed to search for were extremely scarce, and his "essential service" was therefore essentially obsolete. The *W* badge served mainly to intimidate Ukrainian militiamen so that they wouldn't drag him off to the Gestapo, but for the Germans it had no meaning at all, and if they had caught him, he would have been killed. Trusting the certificate was like closing your eyes and believing you were safe because you no longer could see the danger.

In my father's opinion, we were in a potentially more precarious situation than those Jews in hiding, but Mottel insisted we were safe. He said his Gestapo boss, "a gentleman of the old school" who was impeccably dressed and looked like Hitler, had vowed to look after the Sternberg family and tell them when to go into hiding, and that promise now included us, too.

"What if Mottel's Black Shirt is transferred?" my father asked Jan the following night as the two men sat at the barrel table.

"I hear he's a sick man," Jan said of the Gestapo chief. "He was injured in the First World War." Typical of Jan, that answer; he didn't try to calm our fears. The Gestapo protector might be replaced at any time.

Arthur and I lay on the bed. We waited in a hungry stupor for the meal my mother was preparing from a beef bone, root vegetables Jan had brought, and some prunes my father had obtained in barter. A feast.

To distract us as we waited, my mother began to tell of the Friday nights when she was a girl, the only night the entire family sat down for a meal together. The kindling of the Sabbath lights in the silver candlesticks standing on the embroidered tablecloth beckoned everyone to the table. On other nights the table was covered with an ordinary tablecloth. "During the week we sat alone or stood about like a bird on one leg," she said. "But on Friday nights . . ." My mother bit her lip and turned her head away.

Lying next to Arthur on the Sternbergs' cot, my mind reverted to something that had nothing to do with the struggle to stay alive, a turn it had only taken in the recent past when I was sitting with Jan at the little window in the barn. Would that be possible here, I wondered.

Chapter Thirty-three

THE HANDFUL OF Jews with certificates in Skala lived the lives of ghosts. My father went out as seldom as possible. In a sudden random roundup when men were ordered to pull down their pants, not even his *W* would have saved him. Arthur was never permitted to leave the house. My mother was too nervous to go out during the daytime, and at night she couldn't see well enough to find her way around.

That meant I was responsible for organizing food and fuel. On dark nights I made forays into the fields to glean whatever sticks lay about so my mother could cook a little soup. Lately, there hadn't been anything but twigs, and we had no coal, either.

The nights seemed much longer than the days, probably because in the dark afternoons of winter we sat around without light. Even if we had a candle or a bit of kerosene for the lamp, we never kept a light on after seven in the evening, fearing to call the attention of murderers and blackmailers to our presence.

Unnerved by my father's floor-pacing, my mother often told him to stop wearing himself out; besides, she said, he was wasting his energy and there was so little to eat as it was.

Jan's almost daily visits served as relief. The two men spent the time talking in the corner as Jan puffed on a cigarette and my

father watched the smoke slowly fade away. Jan always had lots
to relate: which farmer might be willing to sell me some potatoes,
which Jews had been denounced or had given themselves up,
what war news had filtered down to the Ukrainian militia.

I was hungry for news, but reports on the progress of the war
were unreliable. One day Jan brought a map which we scanned
under the candlelight to figure out the Russians' position.

"Do you hate the Germans as much as I do?" I asked him.

"I hate the misery they cause," was his reply.

During those long months of the winter of 1942–43, Jan and
my father became friends. My father liked him despite the fact
that he was a Ukrainian *goy*—and yet if he hadn't been one,
chances are they'd never have formed a connection.

"Jan, after the war, when we go to Paris, you must come with
us," he said one time.

"Yes, of course," Jan answered. "Do they need eight-fingered
shoemakers there?"

He was still a mystery to me even though I saw him every day.

Most nights, Jan and I went up to the attic; he, the sentinel at
the window, and I, the tower princess. From there, as in Grandfather Jakob's house, there was a view of the marketplace, and
we would be able to warn the others if the Gestapo was coming
for us. I used my shawl as a pillow as I lay on the bare floor.

Our talk mostly concerned the amazing acts people were
capable of in these times. He told me about a peasant whose
house had been set on fire when Jews were found in the cellar.
The man had run into the burning building to try to save them
and had died in the flames. As if tilting a seesaw, he then told
me about a tailor he knew who went to Gestapo headquarters
and denounced a pair of Jewish sisters, old customers of his, for
the reward money. He told these stories matter-of-factly, as if
reading to me from the newspaper, as if they told of occurrences
as natural in the universe as the arrival of night and day.

Sometimes we sat in the dark, he smoking a cigarette, and I,
if the sky was not cloudy, positioned so I could see a patch of
stars. Sometimes we sat on the floor with our backs to the wall,
holding hands. Once in a while, he put his arm around me and

kissed me. That was usually right before he left—a good-night kiss. Once, after he made me laugh, I reached over and kissed him on the cheek and he kissed me back in a way that I liked, but then I pushed him away.

Chapter Thirty-four

I GOT A NEW JOB: laundress at German headquarters on the count's former estate. It was arranged by Shimek's father, who had survived the *aktsia* along with his wife and son, and now worked directly under the protection of the new manager of the estate. Mr. Bosek pointed out to me that this *Obergauleiter*, his German boss, a veteran of the First World War with a glass eye and false teeth, was a man who just wanted to keep things status quo. "He's harmless."

"Let's see your hands," the manager said when I came to see him about the job. He wore a business suit and a tie. He was not much taller than I, and had a pinched look on his face and a dueling scar from mouth to ear. He gestured me to come closer. It was obvious that my soft hands and thin wrists wouldn't be much use at the washboard, but he agreed to let me try. That night my mother coached me on methods of starching collars and removing stains.

The next day, as I scrubbed and rinsed the clothes, water spilled over me and I stood shivering in wet shoes on the stone floor. Ironing was a worse disaster; I scorched one of the detachable white shirt collars and burned my hand. The *Obergauleiter* seemed amused by my ineptitude, but the hard-working Polish girls cursed me. They left the door open on purpose as they went in and out so I'd catch a draft.

The indoor temperature was only slightly less freezing than the air outdoors. The manager noticed my blue, goose-pimpled legs and called me into his office. "Here," he said, holding up a pair of dark-brown cotton stockings. "Put them on."

I turned to go behind the screen. "Put them on here." *Here* meant a chair facing his. I realized this was a condition of the gift. He reached for a glass, fished out a set of false teeth, and popped them in his mouth, making him look somewhat less wizened. His thin face spoke his concentration, as if he regarded my putting on stockings as a particularly difficult puzzle and by watching me he could solve it.

"You have beautiful legs," he said. "Walk around a bit." He sat there as I marched up and down about twenty times, he looking at my brown legs and I not daring to stop. Then he got up and brought a package with a brassiere, garter belt, and panties in it. "Try them on. If they fit they're yours." I told him I had lots of underwear. "But thanks anyway," I said as I edged to the door.

With no sign of a whip or a dog and Mr. Bosek's assurance that the Nazi's bark was manner and not substance, I bade him a quick good night and scooted out the door. The next day I took the brown stockings off when I arrived at the manager's house, fearing he'd make me give them back. "It's cold," he said. "Put the stockings on." Then he walked out of the room.

A short while later, the manager looked at my hands and said, "You're not a washerwoman," and put me to work mending socks and sewing on buttons, which suited my talents better.

Zhenia lived in a tiny room on the estate and I went to see her. I sat on the soft mattress listening to her story.

During the *aktsia*, when our family hid in the egg warehouse, Zhenia had watched from behind the door of her house as the Germans took her widowed mother, grandmother, and uncle away.

Hearing that they had been deported to Belzec, she bribed her way to an audience with the district commander. She asked to be sent to Belzec too. He jumped out of his chair, she said, and picked up his riding crop. When she neither cowered nor batted an eyelash, he put it down again. He was the one who decided, he told her, where she would go and what she would do. Calling her "Jewish whore," he sent her to work as a maid in the German officers' quarters. There, an SS man, defying the nonfraternization rule, set her up in her own little room and provided her with food and clothes.

Knowing her relatives were dead, that they had died before she could have gotten to Belzec, she decided to use her position in the enemy camp to help other Jews.

"Remember how I played Queen Esther one Purim?" she asked me. Yes, I recalled her as Esther. She'd worn a shimmery gown with wide sleeves, and when she extended her imperious arm to accuse Haman, gasps of satisfaction were heard in the audience.

Now, ensconced among Germans, she fed information to a Jew masquerading as a gentile who worked on the premises. "He has contact with the underground," she told me. "What underground?" I asked, and she assured me there was one. Once she realized that she was no longer living under God's protection, she said, she felt great relief. "I have nothing to be ashamed of," she said as she showed me cans of food she had stored to pass on to starving Jews in Skala.

Zhenia, with her usual excited interest in the topic at hand, looked as blooming as ever, and yet, since I knew her so well, I could detect a wilting in progress, as in a plant that sheds random, sere leaves and may never blossom again.

I went to visit her a few more times in her room and each time urged her to search for a hiding place or arrange an escape route for herself through the "passing" Jew. No, she assured me, her Nazi lover adored her, and what sort of Queen Esther would she be if she ran away? "Come share my room," she suggested, offering to set me up with a pal of her SS man.

One time I told her about Jan, how he looked after my family and me, and that I knew he wanted me but that I held back. "Why? For what?" I would have felt foolish saying that it was because he was a *goy*, a shoemaker, ten years older than me, so I said, "He never read a book." Zhenia laughed. "Neither did I."

She told me that if I joined her I could help more people than just my family. "Your guy is small potatoes," she said.

Most mornings Jan came to the house at seven to escort me to the job, and every evening he came around six to pick me up. He took my arm as we left; no one could doubt I was his girl, his presence telegraphing a lay-off policy to his fellow militiamen. To denounce me meant reckoning with Jan.

Once in a while, when I saw some of the girls whispering to each other, I sneaked away to Shimek's house on the estate. His mother always had a spare slice of bread on which she piled sautéed onions. A few times she spread it with honey.

Shimek had a hideout behind the greenhouse, and sometimes I looked for him there. My private grapevine for what was going on in the world, he told me what his father heard on the BBC when the manager was away. He told me about the Russian offensive, and we were jubilant when the Red Army liberated Kiev and then Zhitomir. The following week the Germans retook Zhitomir, but to keep up our spirits we gloried in the constant rain, which was sure to slow the Germans counterattack, perhaps to a halt.

Shimek offered to steal a book for me from the count's library. I declined. He confessed that he couldn't seem to read a book to the end anymore. I told him that his father was foolish to depend completely on the manager and that they should build a hiding place or find one with gentiles out of town. Shimek said that his father didn't trust Ukrainians and that Poles were almost as bad.

"I'm thinking of running away to the forest," he said. "Will you come?"

"Not to the forest."

"Maybe we could join a fighting band."

"If you hear of one, let me know." I had heard about partisan groups, but not of any near our region. Some of them hated Jews more than Germans. I didn't want to tell Shimek that I preferred a quick death by a bullet to starving in a cold dark hole in the ground. Besides, how could I abandon my parents and Arthur?

Shimek got up to peek around the corner of the greenhouse.

"It's because of him, isn't it?" He gestured with his shoulder and head. Jan was standing at the door waiting for me to come out. "Do you love him?"

"Who said I love him?" The annoyance in my voice was clear. "Why do you listen to gossip?"

"All right." He sat down beside me again and kissed me lightly.

It hadn't occurred to me that Shimek might be jealous of Jan. He should have understood that Jan was protecting my family and me. It didn't matter how I felt about him. I said, "Does your mother have to sleep with the manager?" I said it with a brutal hiss that I later realized came from more than the insult he had leveled at me.

Daily the atmosphere of threat settled more heavily over the grounds of the estate, and I felt conspicuous as the only Jew on the domestic staff except for Mr. Bosek. The Polish and Ukrainian men passing through the house looked at me as if to say, "You stupid bitch, you'll get what's coming to you." I had overheard one of the Polish girls saying that it was a "scandal" for a Jewish girl to have the easiest job. Once they hid my sewing box, and when I found it, there was a dead mouse squeezed on the spools of thread. At lunchtime, when the manager and his staff went out to eat, I sat in the back of a broom closet on a pail, hoping Jan would come for me early. Sometimes he did.

One evening, when Jan brought me home, I urged him to come in. He had removed my Jewish-star armband before we crossed town and put it in his pocket. Now he put it back on the sleeve of my coat so that I wouldn't be caught without it the next morning.

"I'm too exposed there," I blurted out to my father and Jan. My father asked Jan if he could arrange a bribe, using two hides he'd hidden with him. The next day Jan showed up at the estate late in the afternoon and announced that I'd been fired.

One night later that winter, Lotka appeared at the back door. With her auburn hair bleached with peroxide to the color of weak lemonade and layered in braids around her head, her green eyes, and her self-confident carriage, she could easily have been taken for a gentile. Her thick eyebrows had been tweezed to crescent shape. She was wearing an embroidered peasant-type fur jacket that her father had sent her with the middleman.

Only the Polish couple she was living with had known of her Jewish identity, and every safeguard had been taken to hide it, but she must have slipped up in some way. A blackmailer had challenged her, and she had barely managed to escape by giving him her last *zloty*.

Her parents bundled her away into their room, but not before I saw the shame in Lotka's eyes, the look of a girl in a bath who suddenly realizes she's being watched.

Jan proposed that I go away with him to Cracow or some other large city. He would get papers from the priest of a neighboring town to show I was Catholic, and all I had to do was learn basic practices and a few prayers. Even though Lotka hadn't succeeded at impersonating an Aryan, I told my father, I was willing to try. But Jan knew as well as I did that I looked Jewish by feature as well as by my "sad eyes," an unmistakable Jewish trait. And I had no *kennkarte* (working papers) to show I had a job.

My father said no. Was it because he couldn't bear to think of us as a couple? In a new city there would have been no one we knew to gossip about me, to say, "Fanya Gottesfeld has a *goy*." To have cared about that seems lunacy to me now. Perhaps it was for another reason: a premonition.

Chapter Thirty-five

ALARMS SIGNALING flash roundups were becoming more frequent. The alarms would come so suddenly that there was no time to get to any of our hiding places and we had to run anywhere we could. It was everyone for her or himself, but my father always carried Arthur.

I remember how he once returned after a false alarm with Arthur crouched low on his shoulders, hands clasped under my father's chin. My mother lifted him off and kissed him and wouldn't let him go for a long time.

Late one night Jan hurried in wearing a jacket over his nightshirt, with boots on but no hat. He ushered us out quickly the back door and wordlessly indicated that my parents and Arthur should lie down on the floor of the wagon, which had a horse tethered to it. Handing me a scarf to tie around my head, he pointed to the seat next to his.

In the predawn light, we pulled up to a house in the countryside where Jan had arranged for us to spend the day in the attic. At noon the householder came up with a bowl of cucumbers and sour cream. Another false alarm.

Late that night, Jan came to lead us home on foot, and I remember the extraordinarily clear night, the stars closer than usual, and how the wide-open road and the fields beyond suggested limitless space. I felt that if we kept walking like this—my father and Jan on either side of me and my mother and Arthur behind us—we'd find an island of safety. And I vowed I'd eat cucumbers and sour cream every day after the war.

By coming to get us at night with the horse and wagon, which could not have gone unnoticed by his mother and sister and brother-in-law, Jan had shown them that he was still a "Jewish uncle."

The people in Father Derewienko's Orthodox church, where he had once been an altar boy and had taken this job very seriously, told him that what he was doing was sacrilegious and a defiance of the church. They made it clear that his absence would be welcomed. "I don't need to go to church to pray," he said when he told me about this.

One Sunday morning when we had scattered in all directions, I ran blindly for a while until I came to the door of a Ukrainian man who had gone to the *gymnasium* with Uncle Wolf. Hat on, ready for church, he motioned me in.

"Please let me stay for a few hours," I pleaded. I must have looked crazy, arriving barefoot, dressed in a nightgown. "Just while you're in church."

He looked at me for a while. An educated man, a high school graduate, a man with whom I had had a few casual but intelligent conversations, a man who lived alone and would put only himself in jeopardy, he stood there interrupting the silence with a few clearings of the throat.

"If they find me, you can say you didn't know I was here." I forced myself to bend my knees to his bare floor.

He shook his head and held the door open. "You killed Jesus Christ," he said. "You people murdered him. Serves you right. I can't sit in church and pray with you here."

That night, while Jan and I kept vigil in the Sternbergs' attic, I quoted the man's words. "That's what the priest told him," he said. "But not all priests would have sent you away." That was true, I knew, remembering the one who had helped Lotka.

"Do you think Jews killed Jesus Christ?" I had wanted to ask Jan this question a number of times.

He took my hand. Very lightly, he rested it on his palm so that what he was saying came through his skin as well as off his tongue.

"I don't know. I wasn't there. Christ was a Jew himself. I have no way of knowing. If they did, it was wrong."

"I don't believe it. Anyway, they can't blame us now." I was close to tears.

He stroked my hand. "They do," he said.

When an alarm a few weeks later galvanized us to run in all directions, we had no time even to grab a blanket. My parents fled with Arthur riding on my father's shoulders.

Jan appeared at our house and led me through back alleys to the bathhouse in my Wasserman grandparents' yard. He hacked away the frozen cover of the hiding place behind the bathtub and we crawled in. Underground, with low headroom, the hole was a tight squeeze for a six-footer like Jan. Lying down was more comfortable than squatting, and Jan gave me his arm as a pillow.

Suddenly severe abdominal pains began to stab me so relentlessly that our lying was more like the writhing of a snake in a death agony than a human embrace.

In the vortex of pain, time-sense abandoned me and place became a surrounding no further than a few inches beyond the body. My consciousness melded with sensation as the waves of agony advanced and receded. I rode those waves in Jan's arms, oblivious that night turned to day and day to night.

I thought I was going to die, that my abdomen had exploded. Violent spasms of diarrhea compounded by menstrual cramps racked my body with the ferocity of labor pains. The blood and feces that involuntarily flowed from me soiled not only me but him. He held me in his arms until I was able to squat over a pail, and then he held me again and again, so that the pail would not tumble over. I concentrated every fiber I could summon on one thing: not to moan or cry, which is what I wanted to do. Tears could be allowed to flow freely, but throat sounds would give us away.

Jan feared that dogs would pick up the pungent human scent. However, for once, the severity of the winter came to our aid. Everything, even odor, froze within a short time, and only the proximity of our bodies kept us in thaw.

When the pains eased somewhat I developed a shudder, a continuous series of shivers that made my teeth clack, and I tried to will my mouth shut.

During the second night, Jan released his hold. I begged him not to go but he left, promising to be back soon. I rolled myself into a ball, sure I'd be dead when they found me.

I don't know how long it was before he lowered himself down next to me again and said, "I made it just in time. It's almost dawn. The *razzia* (raid) is still on. Here, drink this." He lifted a little can with a handle and took off the cover. Milk. It was still lukewarm as I cupped the can in my hands.

He had gone home and heated milk for me and carried it back in the dark.

We must have dozed through that day because it was deep night when we ventured out and he led me back to my parents. Frantic with worry after they had returned from their asylum, they had looked for us in the cellar and garden hiding places and found no trace.

Arthur woke up and approached me. "You stink," he said, and went back to his place on the cot.

From that time on, a new intimacy developed between Jan and me, a closeness that brought him into my inner circle which included my parents and Arthur. Jan had seen me at my worst— he told me later that for a time I groaned like any vile coward— but neither moral weakness nor stench and dirt nor danger of discovery had turned him against me. I trusted him completely.

Some weeks later, my father came back from a tour of hiding places to report that the one in the bathing shed was no longer safe; someone had used it and left a frozen pail of human soil encrusted with blood.

Jan happened to be in the room and kept a straight face.

Chapter Thirty-six

B Y THE TIME spring came around, my father began to feel that our stay with the Sternbergs was becoming too dangerous and our reprieve would soon come to an end. He warned Mottel not to trust his Gestapo boss and not to wait until the last minute to prepare an escape. Mottel insisted that he and his family were safe and that he would be the one to decide if and when it was time to leave town and go into hiding.

My father and Jan, trying to come up with someone who could provide us with a safe hiding place, spent weeks going over the names of gentiles my father had known while in the lumber business and when he'd been an engineer on the Soviets' bridge-repair project.

"Try Sidor," my father told Jan. Sidor, once a worker on the bridge, had moved to Trujca, a village not far away, when he had married Marynka, a Ukrainian woman with a bit of land. Jan agreed to bring him. Of course it would take some time, since Sidor, though poor, had fields to prepare for planting. "At least Fancia," my father told Jan. If Sidor couldn't take the four of us, at least he might be persuaded to take me.

In the meantime, Jan told us he was enlarging the hiding place in the attic of his barn. Whether Jan needed my father's instructions or not I don't know; they enjoyed the collaboration, their heads bent over a crude plan my father drew.

"Watch out for the saw," he told Jan one time. "You can't afford to lose any more fingers."

Jan smiled. "The day you make me a pair of boots I can take five steps in, I'll give you a horse."

They both laughed at the thought of my father with a horse. What use would he have for a horse? "I'll settle for a horseshoe," he said and went back to his design.

It was finally high summer. At the kitchen table, my father and I were trying to guess where the Russians, who had launched a new offensive, might be, as we shifted knives and forks to alter positions on one side of the Dniester River or the other. We heard Jan's knuckle-tattoo on the door.

As he came inside, his face, a mask of furrowed brow, glittering eyes, and tight lips, changed like an actor's to one with relaxed jaw below a smiling mouth, with kind eyes and with his forehead clear. His skin took on a burnished glow that may have been due to the candle's light or to our warm expressions of welcome. Perhaps the look of relief came from being able to put his rifle in the corner and hand us whatever he had to offer.

Tonight, instead of bringing a bit of cheese or matches or a page or two from a newspaper, he plunked a bottle of home-brewed vodka on the table. He had never brought vodka before. Ukrainians hoarded such "essentials" now even more than usual.

My mother put cups on the table for us and a large jar for Jan.

"What do you think I am? A Russian?" He got up and found a small cup on the shelf.

We laughed. We knew that the Ukrainians drank as much as the Russians, maybe more, but Jan's joke also alluded to the fact that the Ukrainians hated the Russians.

"Drink up," my father said, "while we're still . . . healthy." He had wanted to say "alive."

My mother stood up. "Who knows what's going to be tomorrow, if we'll still be here tomorrow, if . . ." She looked over at Arthur asleep on his cot.

I got up. "Come on, let's have a little fun. Let's sing a song. How about the one the Russian officer used to sing?"

"How he loved my gefilte fish!" My mother extended an apologetic look to Jan as if to say, it's not that we're not grateful for the potatoes you bring. Once in a while, when Jan brought potatoes, perhaps an egg, and a little onion, my mother made mock gefilte fish.

"Jan," she said, "after the war you'll taste my fish. And you'll drink tea in a glass in a silver holder."

"Yes," Jan said as he refilled our glasses, "after the war . . ." and he looked as if he could see it somewhere down the road of his glance into space—some point that kept vanishing from our gaze, but when it did we could look at Jan and see that he saw it. He started to sing a song I'd learned by listening to Ukrainian schoolmates, and I sang it with him.

Arthur slept through it all.

What none of us allowed ourselves to think at the time was not that we and Jan could be shot in a few hours, a possibility we couldn't forget—he took his life into his hands every evening when he knocked on our door and handed us something to eat—but that we were sitting around a table drinking like *goyim* with a *goy*. Not even a Pole but a Ukrainian; and not a member of the intelligentsia, but one who was poorly educated, a man who, when he cursed, said, "Holy Mother of God." That expression, something unimaginable, always caught me up short. God had no mother or father.

Jan was someone who would never have been sitting with us in such intimacy before the German occupation. We wouldn't have wanted him, and he would have declined our invitation. The ground rules were broken, and there was a distinct possibility that he would never follow them again.

Jews had always said that the *goyim* hated us. According to my mother, they hated us because we had nicer things than they did; my father believed it was because we were smart and not lazy. Even when we were still living at home, I had countered that there were gentiles who had nicer things than we did and hated us anyway, and that I knew Jews who were dumb and lazy. When I said such things, my parents used to give me an amused look, secretly glad that I had the spirit to contradict them. "That's the way she was under the Russians," my mother said, referring to the time when, as a budding Communist, I had expounded Marxist doctrine with similar conviction. They hadn't believed a word of what I'd said then, nor did I modify their views now.

Late one night I quizzed Jan: "Do you hate me?"

"Would I be sitting here if I did? Do you want me to?"

That wasn't the point. Sometimes, as I lay awake during the night, a peculiar anguish spread over me in a rush, like desire, and I'd think: I want to live. Not I don't want to die, but I want to live, and the "live" echoed like the sound of a coin thrown to the bottom of a well. I wanted to accomplish something before I died, some work in which I'd be of use to others; I wanted to fall in love and to know sex as a pleasure, something more than a kiss or two. I wanted to be kissed and to kiss back. And I wanted my parents and Arthur to live.

Since rumor had become fact, since people were murdered every day, since the *aktsia*, since hiding had become a way of life, I wondered more and more why this was happening to me.

"Why is there . . . ?" I didn't know the rest of my own question.

"You ask questions," said Jan. "I don't have answers. Must you understand?"

"Yes."

"I don't know. One day in the square I saw some Jews pushed into a corner, and one—maybe you know her, the one who wears a red wig; you know her, she had a childhood illness, lost her hair, and didn't find a man until she was thirty . . ."

"You mean Chaya? Chaya the Wig?"

"Yes. Suddenly she's on the ground and screaming. 'The baby,' someone shouted, and I looked again; of course, she was pregnant. Her labor pains had begun. The baby was born in the street. And Stanislaus took the baby and tore it apart.

"I try not to tell you things like this, but you ask me why. Should I say Stanislaus is crazy or that he holds a grudge because a Jew once cheated him? No. He wanted to do it. I went to school with him. He has a good head on his shoulders, he doesn't beat his wife. He goes to church. He wanted to do it, and there's no law against it. He's the law. The law is behind us. Kill. I'm supposed to kill you. And Stanislaus? He'll do it again, given half a chance."

Jan had not spoken like this before. I felt cut and slashed by his words and by his tone, not because it was sharp but because it was so dry, as dry as parched earth. I didn't dare go near him.

In the morning I saw Jan sitting at the window. He hadn't gone home, as usual. I sat down in my spot next to him.

"Can't you talk to Stanislaus? Tell him what he does is . . ."

"No, I do what I can. That's all I can do."

He looked at me. For the first time I saw a look of pity, not because I was a Jew or stupid, but because I talked like a child, an overgrown child who didn't know limits.

He got up. The early sun was bright but not warm. I stretched on tiptoe and kissed him on the cheek to say, Jan, what you do *is* enough. It is enough.

V

Under Sidor's Wing
(August 1943–March 1944)

Chapter Thirty-seven

WITH A THICK SHAWL over my head and paper stuffed between jacket and blouse to keep out the chill of the 1:00 a.m. air, I set out with Jan for Sidor's house in the next village, Trujca. I had decided not to wait another day until he could come to us.

We walked along the river at a swift pace, always alert for the German patrol whose men were stationed in various spots. When we saw Germans we ducked, waiting until a soldier looked away for a moment before going on. The patrol was watching for Jews; the Ukrainians had given the Germans a list of who had been killed or deported and who was still alive, and they knew that the Gottesfelds were still at large.

My swift pace was also due to the animal exuberance released now that I was no longer cooped up. Jan and I almost ran the eight kilometers. I heard the river's flow on my right, and closer by, the hoot of an owl. The novelty of taking great strides, of stretching my steps to fall in with Jan's long-legged ones, flared up into an elation of muscular memory, of opening the throttle for young, vigorous limbs to easily carry me where I wanted to go.

At one point I stumbled on a rut in the road, and as Jan helped me up, he took my hand in his, but I wormed mine out. I didn't need to be shielded. Instead, I covered the three fingers of his left hand with mine. At first he urged me to scoot around and take his right hand, but I told him that the missing fingers didn't bother me. I asked him about the accident. "Water under the bridge," he replied evasively.

My father had instructed me to stay at Sidor's for a few days and gauge the situation: what kind of person Sidor's wife was—could she be trusted? and would their little girl, who was Arthur's age, blab to neighbors that Jews were hiding in the house? and was there enough space for the four of us? and if so, to persuade Sidor to let us come.

Jan planned to stay with me all three days, a safer course than being seen going back and forth. While there he would do some work around the house, so that the neighbors would find his presence normal and natural in the future.

"How do you know they will let me stay on?" I asked him.

"Because I know Sidor," he said. Jan had once repaired a harness for Sidor in the days when the peasant had owned several cows and a horse, and he had spent several days there convincing Sidor to shelter us. Jan's talking of Sidor's one thin cow—"You can look straight through her"—muffled the sounds of approaching feet.

It was a German patrol.

Its leader kicked Jan in the ribs. I could feel the blows in my body because Jan had thrown me to the ground and himself on top and was grinding his hips into mine.

"What are you doing?" the patrol leader demanded.

"What does it look like?" Jan answered. A few of the men laughed in a raucous way. We heard their joking as they wandered down the road.

After they left, a twinge of fear ran through me. What if they had seen me, seen my Jewish face? What if, what if—useless what if. We had to be more careful. Hands clasped, we adopted a steady pace.

When we finally arrived at the house, entering it through a dark doorway, Sidor directed us to a little alcove separated from the main room by a thin curtain over its small opening. We collapsed onto the bench, which had some pillows on it.

After what seemed like a few hours of dead sleep, Sidor woke us at dawn and beckoned us to come sit at the table. I looked around the kitchen; it had a stove, a bed where Sidor, Marynka, and their little girl all slept together, a small wardrobe, and a few stools. Everything—cooking, eating, sleeping—was carried on in this one room.

Marynka sat on the bed, drawing on thick stockings. She resembled the fiancée Jan had brought to our house: robust figure, Slavic high cheekbones, and pug nose. Her braided blond hair, though not thick, framed her face to advantage. I could see what had attracted Sidor: she held herself in the self-possessed way that a pretty woman does, and only her gold-lined front tooth, which glistened when she smiled, marred her good looks. (Jan later told me that Ukrainians thought it beautiful, a sign of prosperity.)

Sidor, a stocky man with black eyes and close-cropped hair who was shorter than Marynka, had a serene expression on his face. But when Marynka came over to the table to slice some bread, I could see that she wasn't happy to have us there. Still, she cut each slice equally and wrapped up a few in a piece of cloth for the three of them to eat at the market in another town where they were going that morning.

Their little girl, Hania, was blond like her mother and dark-eyed like her father. She rubbed her eyes and hid partway behind Sidor, then looked me over.

I was still wearing the last ring we had, a gold band set with one large and one small garnet. My father had instructed me to give it to Marynka. It was hard to part from this ring, a birthday gift from my father, but I took it off my finger and put it in her hand. Marynka tried to put it on one finger after another by greasing the inner rim with lard, but it would not slide on, not even on her pinkie. She knotted it into the end of her handkerchief and put it in her blouse.

Before leaving for the market, Sidor warned me not to go near the window or open the door, not to cook, and to use the slop pail instead of the outside privy. He told Jan to make a bed for us in the attic and, taking Hania's hand, said they would be back at nightfall. Marynka turned as she left, and her half-smile made me uneasy.

She's Ukrainian, Jan explained to me after they left, and Sidor is a Pole, not a common combination. I asked if he was as good-tempered as he appeared to be. "In the morning," Jan said, "he gets out of bed on the right side and Marynka on the wrong side. What a couple!"

In the attic, Jan shook a mound of straw and I helped spread it. Then he made a twin for it. The straw had a sun-musk smell. For a change, Jan didn't position himself at the window, and he came to lie down next to me.

Chapter Thirty-eight

LATER THAT MORNING, in the snug burrow of that straw bed, Jan and I made love for the first time. It took a long time. Gentle Jan. I prayed it would always be as it was for us that day—losing track of time as we caressed each other, our airy bodies pressing and rocking high over the top of the world.

A thick, warm ray of sunshine came in through the small square window of the attic and warmed the small of my back. "I'm glad it's daylight," said Jan. "You're beautiful." Lying there with Jan, I felt I was.

The next day, resting in Jan's arms, I found myself crying and spilling happy tears. Love-making surprised me: it felt so right, the only right thing in a time of madness. All awkwardness had left me. Jan, this most unlikely partner, felt right. Somehow I had imagined that he would feel heavy, but there was no sense of crush, only lightness and light.

"Why are you astonished?" Jan asked.

"I just am," I said.

With refreshed sight, the ordinary view from the window of the late-fall meadow appeared entrancing; my fingers stroked fabric, wood, metal as if learning touch for the first time; and at times my breasts and my inner places announced themselves as if brushed by a satin glove.

I tried to keep busy over the next few days by sweeping the floor and washing the dishes. No use. Even after I jumped up and down a hundred times, sudden elation overtook me. I longed for dejection, the familiar dark mood that had enveloped me since the coming of the Germans. I had to summon dread consciously from where it had taken a back seat. My pleasure, I was thinking, could lead to our destruction; in this high mood I could be lying in Jan's arms instead of listening for the sounds of German motors and dogs.

I made a mental list—there was no paper or pencil in the house—of the reasons I should despise myself: I had consented to intimacy with a *goy*—a Ukrainian! Not a doctor or a member of the intelligentsia—but a shoemaker! A man ten years older than I, a rifle-carrying member of the militia. Although Jan's affection for me was clear, he had exerted no pressure on me to become his lover. It appeared to have just happened. I had no one to blame but myself.

Yes, I had remembered my father's injunction, "Be nice to him." But now I feared his anger. Had he meant for me to go this far? My mother, I knew, wouldn't say a word but would give me pitying looks. A few years before, during a comfortable chat when I admitted liking a certain boy in my class, she had told me to remain friends, nothing more; to wait until I got married. Then she recounted the horrible nights of her honeymoon. It hadn't been that way for me. It had been sweet, and I hated myself for wanting more. Despite my anxiety, my heart had expanded to include an additional tenant, Jan, and to him it opened a private, forbidden room.

During the next few days, when Jan was repairing Sidor's window frames, I had time to try to gather my wits. I was in the country but could not step out the door. Jan and I drank fresh milk while my family starved in Skala. Sidor was sheltering me today but might denounce me tomorrow.

At an odd moment, it occurred to me that Sidor had said "Make a bed," not "beds," and Marynka's half-smile as she left might have been an insinuation that she knew how we would spend the day. Perhaps Jan had made an arrangement with Sidor. Anything was possible. These were murderous times. The first priority was for Jan to see that I was safe.

Chapter Thirty-nine

ON THE THIRD MORNING of our stay, Marynka was adamant: I could come live with them, I could help her with the housework, and if Jan brought wool, I could earn my keep by knitting sweaters she could sell to other peasants. But she would not consent to having my parents and Arthur, too.

"Too dangerous," said Marynka. In the neighboring village, a man who had sheltered Jews had seen his wife and children shot in front of his eyes. Then he was tied up within sight of their corpses, which everyone was forbidden to remove and bury.

Sidor tried to persuade Marynka to give the whole family a try by saying that my father had done him some favors and was willing to give them whatever we had. God knows, they could have used any contribution we made. I could see they were very poor: a few cooking utensils, a few tattered quilts, a little trunk, summed up their household goods.

Looking out the window, I watched a few scrawny chickens run between the legs of a cow so undernourished she barely gave milk. Not even one pig was in the pen. The one old horse they had was all skin and bones, and limped. Their tiny field did not grow enough food for them to be self-sufficient—let along feed four additional mouths. Anything we could give them would be used toward seed for sowing an early field of wheat in the spring or for more chickens.

"She can stay," Marynka said to Sidor, gesturing toward me with her head, "but keep your hands off of her." Sidor looked at Jan, whose face remained impassive. Suddenly it was clear whom I belonged to. Perhaps Jan had made love to me to protect me from Sidor. Maybe he didn't love me, just wanted to see that no harm came to me for my father's sake.

Sidor's respect for my father became the coin I decided to trade on to persuade them to accept my parents and Arthur. I told him that my father was a man of his word; after the war he would reward Sidor splendidly, and we had rich relatives in Paris. Marynka scoffed at my assurances. "Promises," she said to Sidor. "In the meantime we don't have enough to eat. Do you want to take the food out of your child's mouth?" Hania looked up at her father, expecting an answer, but he turned away.

Late in the evening, we sat around the table drinking the vodka Jan had saved for our last talk, and Marynka brought some leftovers to go with it.

I told them that the mania to rout out the last Jews had reached fever pitch, with neighbors searching every possible byway and bunker for hidden Jews. Jan added that Uzbek deserters from the Red Army had joined the hunt. When the Ukrainian militia went to search for Jews, "no stone remains unturned," he said.

Sidor and Marynka looked bewildered. It meant searchers would come here, too.

Then Jan told them about what had happened to Dr. Steuerman, who had once relieved Sidor's agony during a gallbladder attack. The doctor had been hiding in a bunker under the Strusover Synagogue in Skala with his wife and daughter and a young woman who had run away from the Borszczow ghetto and had become his lover. The Germans drove the four of them out of the hiding place and gunned them down on the sidewalk. Then the Ukrainians stripped off their clothes. They put Dr. Steuerman's naked body on top of his lover's and left the two of them on the street for days. Ukrainians and Poles came from far and wide to see this "exhibit," laughing at the sight and spitting on the corpses.

"I liked him," said Marynka. "May God have mercy on his soul."

"If you don't let me bring them tomorrow," Jan said, "it will be too late."

Sidor agreed. I took his hand as if to kiss it, but he turned mine and shook it instead.

Marynka walked over to the bed. Kneeling in front of a picture of Jesus on the cross tacked to the wall above it, she began to pray.

Chapter Forty

THAT NIGHT, past 4:00 a.m., Jan left me at the Sternbergs' door. As I groped my way toward the cot I shared with Arthur, I heard a match being struck and I saw my father's face lit up by the candle. He had been sitting in the dark waiting up for me.

I'll never forget the hurt look on his face. The corners of his mouth were drawn in so that he looked as if he might burst into tears. It meant that he knew I had been intimate with Jan. But how did he know? Perhaps my ruddy color or the sixth sense of a loving father told him. Maybe it was because I looked different. The tension born of fear of what was going to happen between Jan and me was now gone. And I had become a woman.

"Where have you been so long?" he asked.

I eased my shoes off and let them drop to the floor. "There's a full moon. We had to go the long way 'round by the woods."

After Jan calculated that the patrol had passed, we had taken a shortcut from behind Sidor's house that led to some fields. In the bracing air, my tightly wound nerves had room to explode and I had started to run. We ran together, this time not from the patrol but toward a small clump of trees which would receive us like a friend.

I looked for traces of pine needles on my sleeves but there were none. I felt devaluated under my father's gaze, undeserving of his vigil.

My mother lay on the bed next to Arthur's, her headache compress in place, her red eyes staring into the void. Tears ran down her rigid cheeks.

"What happened?" I asked. She remained immobile, silent.

The next night, Jan came back to bring my parents to Sidor's. He promised to come get Arthur and me the following night.

Just before we parted, my mother gave me her favorite sweater, a beige cardigan with brown stripes and wooden buttons. Through the window, I watched my father and mother walk down the street, a few small parcels of clothes—the only "possessions" they had left—in their hands.

As I looked out, I saw the darkness envelop them and prayed they would evade the German patrol. Earlier, I used to pray that the soldiers would fall off the riverbank and drown. If there were fewer Germans, I had more chance to live, an elemental premise of war. Now, schooled by the idea that my life would have an early end, I decided that the drowning of a handful of Germans wouldn't save me, that bloodthirst assuages nothing—it didn't even diminish my fear.

With nothing to do the next day but wait for Jan to come pick us up, I started to unravel a sweater of Arthur's that he had outgrown and began a new one for Marynka. Perhaps Jan could get me a bit of wool to add to it.

The next night, Jan came to get us. I wore in layers the few items of clothing I still owned—dresses, a shirt, and a blouse—and carried my mother's sweater on my arm. Jan carried Arthur piggy-back. Soon the rocking motion put him to sleep. We walked at a brisk pace until I pulled into a strolling tempo.

"My parents know," I said. "They were waiting up for me when I got home."

"What did they say?"

"Nothing. My mother was crying. And my father, well, I could tell by his face."

"That's not the reason." He stood still and held my arm to keep me from going on. "I have something to tell you."

While he and I were at Sidor's, he said, someone had come to tell my parents that Grandfather Jakob and Grandmother Miriam had been murdered in the final liquidation of the Borszczow ghetto. That, I now understood, was why my father had decided we had to leave immediately for Sidor's instead of holding off on going to this shelter until the last possible moment. That moment, he had realized, had now come: more mass murders were about to take place.

Jan sat me down in a ditch by the side of the road and let me cry in his arms. "Why didn't they tell me?" I repeated over and over.

It was too cold and too dangerous to stay in one spot. We got up, and as we walked, Jan told me the rest of the story.

Jakob and Miriam had lived with nine other people in one room in the ghetto. The constant fear of a *razzia*, the starvation rations, the constant harassment for contributions by the *Judenrat*, and the spreading contagion of typhus and typhoid must have brought them to the end of despair. They had no money for bribes with which to buy their freedom, no chance of escaping to the forest, no Jan to look after them. And they were in their sixties.

When the alarm reached them, they rushed to their hiding place in the cellar. Grandmother Miriam and some other people managed to get in, but by a fluke Jakob was caught outside. As the Ukrainians dragged him off, he broke away. Running to a German officer, he fell to his knees and offered to tell where Jews were hiding if his life was spared. A red scarf was tied around his neck and he led them to the hiding place, calling: "Miriam, it's safe. You can come out."

As the trapdoor opened from inside and people crawled out, the Germans kicked and beat them, with Jakob looking on.

They were taken out of town with the rest of the Jews, forced to dig a pit, ordered to undress, lined up, and shot row upon row into the pit.

Before long the pit was overflowing with blood, and a deeper one had to be dug.

Before her death, Miriam knew that her husband had led the Germans to the bunker. She saw him standing there among the

Germans and the Ukrainian militia, who forced him to watch the shootings.

Then the German officer came up to him, gun in hand, saying, "This is how we repay traitors," and shot him in the mouth.

Jan knew all the details; I didn't ask him how he knew— perhaps from some other Ukrainians who had been there to loot, rob, and see the big event first-hand.

As we walked on, I suddenly realized that I'd lost my mother's sweater, and I began to cry as if someone I loved had died. Nothing Jan said brought me any comfort. He became upset that I was so distraught. Strange: here I was, running for my life; I had learned that my grandparents were dead, and the sweater was the only thing I could think of. Later, Jan went back across the fields and searched for it, but it was gone.

Chapter Forty-one

SIDOR WAS KNEELING in front of the crucifix over the bed saying his Paternoster. Illiterate, he garbled words he'd learned only by listening to them over and over. "Our Father, who art in heaven . . ." It was the first day the four of us were together in his house.

He then took Hania on his knee and told her that my parents were her uncle and aunt, and Arthur and I her cousins, only it was a big secret and she mustn't tell anyone that we were living in the house. Marynka came over, hairbrush in hand, and undid the child's braids. The girl, stolid as a wardrobe, never flinched or said "Ouch" as her mother yanked the hair into strands and, digging with a fine-tooth comb as if it were a rake, scourged the child's head for lice.

As Marynka worked, she warned Hania not to mention us at school or to the priest. And Hania never did; in fact the only time I heard her speak of us was to Rex, the family's alert German shepherd, during a rainstorm when he was allowed in the house to dry off in front of the stove. "Don't tell," she warned the dog, "or I'll slice you up and put you in the soup."

That evening, I began to teach Sidor the words of the Paternoster. During the morning prayers in Polish elementary school, when I and the other Jewish students sat silently on the sidelines, the words had etched themselves into my memory.

Marynka said that Sidor should be ashamed to take lessons from a Jew, that God knew what he meant no matter how he said it. But Sidor took my efforts as a sign that I deserved protection. My parents concealed their pain when they heard me say the prayer. God, my mother said, would "wash the words off my tongue" since there was no faith behind them.

We settled into the attic, which we reached via a ladder from an unused room filled with straw across from the entrance hall. The attic was small—we couldn't stand, and we could only barely sit in a crouching position.

When it was time for the evening meal, Sidor closed the shutters, as he would do many times in the next weeks, and called us down from the attic. Marynka set on the table a steaming bowl of potatoes and gravy or soup made of whatever vegetables and grain she threw into the pot on the back of the stove. On market days, she added a few scraps of meat or a bone, but after our first few weeks there, such luxury was seldom repeated. Plain though it was, Sidor invited us to share their bounty, and his good-natured presence in the house had a cheering effect on me.

But it was a different story with my mother. During the first few meals, she sat at the table pressing her lips together when her turn came to dip her spoon in the communal earthenware bowl. By the end of the meal, Sidor's glare had fixed on her.

My father and I thought that agitated nerves were preventing her from eating. We tried to persuade her to take some food. It wasn't kosher, my father remonstrated, but so what, God would forgive.

On the third day, she consented to try a spoonful and immediately ran to the slop pail to vomit.

Marynka interpreted this as a comment on her cooking. She hadn't noticed that my mother had spent an hour scrubbing the tin cup attached with string to the water pail. The cup, bent and battered, had kissed so many mouths and acted as ladle for so many brews that no amount of elbow grease could alter its blackened complexion. My mother used her hands as a cup to hold water to drink from the pail.

Later, when I went up to the small space under the attic eaves where my parents lay on a straw bed, my mother admitted that it was disgust that had twisted her stomach into knots. She had seen Marynka wash bed linen, floor rags, and clothes in the bowl we all ate soup from. Nobody in the house used toilet paper. Peasants, my mother explained, didn't wear undergarments, so that when Marynka menstruated, not all of the flow was caught by the tail of the shirt she tied between her legs, and she had seen a trail of blood on the floor. The blood-spotted shirt, too, had had a turn in the bowl.

My father, who used to have to "walk on his hands," as he put it, in order not to muddy the immaculate carpet at home, shook his head. "Stupid woman," he screamed at her, "if you are going to be alive it won't matter. And if you're going to be dead it won't matter." He called her "stubborn" and despaired of reasoning her out of not eating. After five days of refusing food, she gave in.

Early in the fall, on the day she calculated to be Yom Kippur, my mother did not eat from sundown to sundown. Said my father, "God understands this is no time to fast." Neither hunger nor his words budged her. Sidor allotted her an extra piece of bread when she broke her fast, since it had been a religious observance.

Chapter Forty-two

I T DIDN'T TAKE ME LONG to get used to my surroundings; after all, it had been a long time since we owned a bar of soap or a cache of food. Even the odor of the house, a mix of coal, when there was any, and unwashed bodies—neither Sidor nor we ever bathed—and stewing beans or cabbage, a country cottage smell which continued to make my mother nauseous, had in my nostrils the scent of safety.

Once Hania brought home a bunch of daisies she'd picked, and I, sitting near the beaker that held them, enjoyed the atavistic sensation of walking through a meadow on a Saturday afternoon stroll near the ruins of the Turkish Tower. "In another life," the refrain kept repeating in my head: "another life, another life."

Time became telescoped into alarms or, so far, false alarms, with expanses of sick apprehension in between. Every act, every move from chair to bed—taking care not to pass too close to the window—every gesture of courtesy or greed involving another appeared magnified: life or death. It wore us out, the constant tap on the shoulder.

Our lives depended on Marynka's whims. She had assigned me to knit sweaters and stockings from homespun wool which she then bartered for food. During the day, sitting in the half-light near the small window of the attic, I could count the rows, but once it got dark I'd lose count and sometimes drop stitches. Marynka bought a pair of needles for herself so that I could teach her fancy patterns and she could then show off her skill to the neighbors. My father couldn't persuade her that this sudden proficiency would arouse suspicion.

Sidor and Marynka had a next-door neighbor, a Ukrainian bachelor she had her eye on. When Sidor was out drinking at an inn, she would invite the neighbor to come drink with her in the kitchen. And when she was drunk, she sat on his lap. Crouching in the attic, we would hear noises and laughs and movements, and we felt frightened.

One of the sweaters I had knitted she dyed yellow and traded for a new white shirt embroidered in the peasant style. She wore it to church one Sunday. Sure enough, this bachelor neighbor came by the house that evening, on the excuse of wanting to borrow a bit of flour, and we barely had time to scamper up to the attic before Marynka opened the door.

From that day on, we remained in the attic except for an hour or so late at night when we came down to walk up and down on the earth floor, hard except for squishy spots where water or the slop pail had spilled. During the day, while Marynka and Sidor were away in the fields, we ate the piece of bread doled out to us in the morning. Some days, neither Sidor nor Marynka filled the drinking pail at the well, and I was tempted to dip my finger in the soup for a drop of moisture. Marynka would surely notice; I redirected my thoughts to rainstorms and flooding riverbanks. Sometimes my thirst increased, but it was better than risking Marynka's curses. We gave Arthur a morsel of our rations, but a spoonful of kasha is hard to divide into portions.

The discomforts of hunger—gnawing emptiness, headache, dizziness, disorientation, all familiar sensations since the Germans had come—would have been easy to disregard with a distracting activity, but I had nothing to do but clack my knitting needles together when wool was obtainable.

Having almost nothing to eat for days at a time, we became obsessed with food, an engrossing subject that served as an alternative to the constant anxiety about falling into the hands of the Gestapo. My father recalled meals he'd eaten in student cafes in Czernowitz, and my mother dropped all vestiges of a delicate, pious nature when she had the chance to fish a bit of pork bone out of the soup with her fingers or eat some of a chicken that Marynka had found lying dead on the road, a delicious hit-and-run victim.

My mother could sit for hours without moving, but my father's natural restlessness plagued him. He was a veteran floor-pacer, but in the attic there was no room to stand up straight or walk up and down. He had to content himself with shifting his buttocks or shaking his feet.

His university education at Czernowitz passed across his memory as if pages were displayed on an ever-replenished lectern and he sat reading them off to us. He spared us algebraic formulas but reeled off long portions of history, novels, and poems in Yiddish, Polish and German, his voice lowering and filling with vibrato when he came to romantic and philosophical passages. Though no longer the pious believer he'd been as a young man, he recited portions of the Torah he had read aloud when called to the podium in the synagogue.

The Torah extracts did not necessarily occur on Saturday mornings. Calendar time had become superfluous. If Marynka went to church, we knew it was Sunday, but when the weather was fine she and Sidor went out to work in the fields on that day and only took a few hours off in the afternoon. With a nail or stick I began to scratch the mark of each day on the wood of the eaves, and on the seventh, I'd slant a line across the previous six with a satisfying finality that I knew to be false. The seventh day, like a paper calendar page, neither ended nor began anything.

As we neared the end of good weather and early traces of winter became an unspoken fact, I'd catch a look on my father's face as if to say: "You, if only you make it through . . ." He'd mention aunts and uncles in Paris, and I knew that he meant I must get there and tell them what had happened. My father's stance—to take what comes and go on from there, to avoid wasting time and energy by bemoaning our circumstances, not to curse God for turning away from us, above all to keep trying to stay alive—became my posture, too.

Chapter Forty-three

IN THE EARLY-MORNING DARKNESS, even before he arose to light the lamp and she to add wood to the embers in the stove, Sidor and Marynka began to bicker.

Marynka cursed Sidor in Ukrainian for the danger hanging over them since "his" Jews had arrived, and he bombarded her with Polish insults learned during his years in the army. Dumb, she called him, ignorant; she reminded him that he could barely write his name. His shout of regret that he had ever signed his name to their marriage papers roused her fury, and she threatened to report us if he didn't manage to get some dividend from us. Where were our clothes, our furniture, our gold?

We had come to Sidor's with about $250 in glued-together and ironed American bills. Each of us had some of them sewn into our clothing from the days of the German occupation, in case we got lost or separated from the others. Mine were inside my bra, and once, when we were still at home, they had gotten wet when I washed; Arthur's were in his undershorts and little jacket.

My father took the bills from us when we got to Sidor's and doled them out to him one at a time, cautioning him to be careful when he exchanged a bill to buy food, kerosene, and candles. A bedsheet bartered for a small bag of flour would go unnoticed, but a five-dollar bill was a red flag. In the anonymity of a city or large town, it was possible to convert money, but in the nearby villages everyone knew that Sidor and Marynka had next to nothing. And why would a supposedly self-sufficient peasant have to buy food instead of just kerosene and a little salt like the others—and where had he gotten the bills?

When there had been nothing in the soup pot but water and some old turnip peels for several days, my father gave Sidor our last five-dollar bill. At the market, Sidor reported, he was teased about his sudden riches. My father feared that someone would come nosing around to see if Sidor was sheltering Jews.

That night, we took our blankets and slept in the barn. Sidor felt contrite for not managing to change the bill without being noticed. I could hear it in the way he told us he'd bring us food twice a day and change our pails.

The next evening, the bachelor neighbor came to call, on the pretext of having heard there was a cow for sale. Sidor told him no, his cow was old, gave no milk, and wasn't worth her fodder. Sidor distracted him with vodka and he didn't come out to the barn.

Marynka, when she came to bring us back into the house the next day, said it had been a close call.

Jan, slipping in and out at odd hours, brought the only relief. He almost always arrived with some food—cornmeal or a sausage or some cheese. None of us would touch the food until Sidor, Marynka, and Hania came home to share it with us.

One night, Jan was searched by a German patrol on the lookout for smugglers. He explained the hunk of butter he was carrying as being a gift to a married mistress whose name he couldn't divulge, and the German newspaper, which he couldn't read, as cigarette paper.

When he was caught again, he earned a beating and a warning that he'd be taken to headquarters next time. Even the Germans knew by now that he was a "Jewish uncle" and that he was hiding Jews somewhere.

On some visits, Jan would bring nothing but bad news. Ferreting Jews out of hiding places had not lost momentum. One time when Sidor and Marynka were not in the room, he named a peasant who had killed his Jews when their money ran out and left their bodies lying in the fields. We weren't paying Sidor and Marynka for our upkeep, and now our contributions for supplies had run out. My father asked Jan why he had made a secret of the neighbor's action. Surely everyone knew. "Probably," Jan said. It wouldn't matter if Sidor knew, but Marynka, well . . . why put the knife in her hand?"

None of us trusted Marynka, least of all Jan. He would sit with her at the table for hours when he came to see us, eating the eggs she had put aside for him and parrying her flirtatious remarks. He played her game at the beginning because he wanted her to be good to us and knew that this was part of the price he had to pay her for letting us stay.

Marynka would ask when Jan was coming, and as she spoke, her front tooth rimmed with gold would catch the light from the lamp. She would always sponge herself with nice soap and put on her beautiful embroidered white peasant blouse, bleached in the sun, over a long wide skirt. Only boots were missing from her costume, and she longed for them as for a loved one.

As consolation, she'd put around her neck my mother's gold chain with a gold heart pendant that had on it all the marks of our teeth from when Arthur and I had bit into it as children. But she kept the pendant, which my father had given her when he and my mother came to live at the house, tucked inside her blouse. Sidor forbade her to sell my gold ring with the garnets no matter how little food remained in the cupboard.

Chapter Forty-four

ONE NIGHT, when Sidor had taken Marynka to her parents' house in another village along with Hania, I dawdled near the stove in the dark after my parents and Arthur went up to their straw beds in the attic.

Suddenly Sidor slipped in the door. He told me that his wife and child had decided to stay the night. Without lighting a candle, he brought the all-purpose tumbler to share a bottle of vodka with me. It was less than half full. When I declined to drink, he muttered something about my thinking myself "too good" to stoop to drink with a peasant. I denied it and took a sip.

After a while, when I sensed he would soon doze off, I got up. In one lunge, Sidor was up and pressing himself against me. "A Jewish beauty," he said. I pushed him off, but he kept coming back. Locked in the vise of his arms, I thought of biting him, but he let go.

"Don't tell Jan," he said, sitting down hard. Sidor was obviously frightened that Jan would kill him if he knew he'd touched me. He tried to say more, but a sob stuck in his throat. I had the impulse to comfort him but turned and climbed up to my bed.

"Don't tell Jan"; in the old days he would have been afraid I'd tell my father.

My parents had never let on when they first realized Jan and I were lovers. They treated us at Sidor's as they had before: the young people. Young people stay up late. We always waited a decent interval during which they would have time to fall asleep in the attic before we lay down on the bench in the little alcove downstairs. Each morning, after Jan left at dawn, I expected my father to be sitting there waiting as I parted the alcove curtain, to stab me with a look. It never happened.

A word, even a reproving word, from my mother would have been welcome. I wanted to tell her that Jan was very gentle, careful not to rush me, passion so well anointed with affection that during those first three days of our intimacy I could not say precisely when I had stopped being a virgin.

"Lost my virginity." That's how my parents would have put it, but I didn't feel loss; no, I felt that I'd become a woman, gaining the full intelligence of my body, its capacity to respond, to invent, and to send to Jan's body waves of devotion that came as partner to sensations of pleasure. Intense, furtive, filled with tenderness is the way I think of the hours Jan and I managed to spend together.

But even these moments of peace were freighted by fear when he got up to leave. A faceless baby floated in my imagination. Each week after Jan's visit, I'd see the floating baby in my dreams. A child, once the greatest blessing, had become the greatest misfortune. The floating baby was my death warrant. Even if I had the strength to carry it, I would have to go off by myself to have it and get rid of it. A crying baby! I often thought of Wolf and Malcia's whimpering child sick with diphtheria during the *aktsia*. The baby could have given us away or been suffocated. For me to become pregnant would mean the end of all of us because I would no longer be able to help save my family.

I wished I could talk to my mother about ways of not getting pregnant. Jan had said this was his responsibility. In a dark corner of my mind I knew that wasn't true, but short of refusing to sleep with him, I didn't know what to do. I wondered how my mother had managed to have only two children. By putting on her headache compress? Here in hiding, of course, her periods had stopped—starvation had taken care of that.

I thought once or twice about asking Marynka. People who live in the country know about such natural things as a matter of course, though their information is often twisted by superstition. But I was convinced she would laugh at me. I had to rely on my own instincts, decide each thing as it came up.

Jan said I could trust him. And I did. He didn't want me to die. I knew it by the way he held me in his arms. And now that I knew how it felt to be loved, I didn't permit myself any stray, let-come-what-may thoughts. No. I wanted to live more than ever. I had bitten into the apple and found it sweet.

Yet in the eyes of God and my parents, we were sinners. I glanced at my father at casual moments, during one of our scanty meals or during a game of chess that he played solo, using a chess set he had made from rocks and straw, and I saw a suffering look, the pain I was causing him. The rebuke on my father's face haunted me; it took root in my dreams. His look, as if he were staring at an injured bird, belied his soothing voice as he said, "In Paris no one will know. You'll be clean, I promise you."

I didn't feel dirty or wounded during those hours when Jan's arms were around me in the alcove, but I couldn't say that to my father.

I couldn't explain to him that there was something between Jan and me that transcended the physical: we had been allied, entwined, intimately involved with each other for over a year before we made love. Nor could I explain to him—or to myself— why in a hidden corner of my heart I felt maidenly and inviolate.

My periods had become irregular, then stopped, and when some spotting began again I couldn't wait to whisper the news to my mother. Look, I was saying, I'm healthy, I'm not starving. "A gift," she said to her wayward daughter. "The dear Lord has sent you an abortion." I hadn't realized that she thought I'd become pregnant each time I'd been with Jan.

She told me to say a prayer of thanks to God.

Chapter Forty-five

J AN ARRIVED ON SUNDAY on a surprise visit with a request from Rose Bradler, the daughter of the family I'd roomed with as a high school student in Borszczow. She was now hiding with her baby not far from us. Her milk had dried up and she needed sugar for the infant. To give birth to a baby in these times, no matter how foolish or inevitable, was simple compared to finding someone to hide the two of them.

I looked at no one, just watched my mother untie a few lumps of sugar from the corner of a ragged handkerchief. With our last coin, Sidor had procured a bit of sugar for the tea leaves Jan had brought.

"If we give her, we won't have any," my father said. "No, the answer is no." My father, known for his charitable heart by Jew and gentile, told Jan to tell Rose that we had no sugar, that we too were starving. "Tell her we'll send sugar when we have some." Jan nodded without looking up. "And see if you can find a little milk for her." Jan's eyebrows went up as if to say, Easier said than done, but he said nothing.

My mother poured hot water over the tea leaves in the pot for Sidor, Marynka, and Hania, who were expected back from church soon, retied the few broken sugar lumps, and put the handkerchief in her pocket.

Another time Jan brought a letter from my father's sister Sophia, asking if we could arrange to have her, Zygmunt, and Dolek stay with us at Sidor's. They were being sheltered by a peasant, Wasil, in a village a few kilometers from us. Sophia and Dolek had gone to Wasil's right after the *aktsia*, and Zygmunt, who was still in the *Ordnungsdienst*, slept in our house when we lived with the Sternbergs and brought them food every weekend. He subsequently joined them. Now, they said, they expected to be turned out at any minute because their funds were almost gone. My father sent back word with Jan to search for another place, adding pessimistically that we might all "meet at the river" before long, meaning that we'd all commit suicide together rather than be captured and have our bodies mutilated.

Another letter came via Jan from Lolla's sons. It said that Lolla herself could not write because she had been stabbed in the head by the same Ukrainian peasants who had killed her husband in the fields where they were hiding after the *aktsia*. The part of her brain which controls writing was damaged. Lolla, whom my father had felt so close to because she was an intellectual like him, could no longer read or write.

Her sons asked my father if the three of them could come stay with us. My father asked Sidor, who replied that if they came, we would all have to leave. He chose to save his own children and sent back word to Lolla: it was impossible for her and the boys to hide at Sidor's.

The forest, in my father's opinion, was not an option for us. According to Sidor and Jan, people hiding in forest bunkers had to scrounge for food on night forays to distant cottages and were frequently dragged away to the Gestapo.

When I mentioned to my father the possibility of finding a partisan group, I touched off an explosion. "In the forest," he said, "the partisans themselves are the greatest menace." Frustrated by lack of supplies and limited military success, the avowedly anti-Semitic partisans massacred fleeing Jews.

When I asked Jan about fighters in the forest he said my father was right. "How can they fight if they have no arms and nothing to eat?" he asked. Seeing my disappointment he added: "To the west, yes, but not around here." For an instant I doubted them both, yet not enough to take off by myself and find out.

I thought of Shimek. "Maybe Jewish partisans?"

"Dreams," my father said. "In Palestine maybe, but not here."

At the end of Jan's next visit, while we sat waiting for the last rays of light to disappear, he handed me a letter. It was from Shimek. He had given it to Ulanowski, whom he had met through my father before the war and who kept in touch with us via Jan or Sidor.

Jan admitted that he'd been carrying the letter around for weeks but couldn't bring himself to deliver it. Jealousy, he said; he had been jealous of my feelings for Shimek. I asked him how he knew what I felt. "The way you looked at him in your garden." Ancient history. Those days when Shimek and I sat on a bench talking about a book we'd read seemed to belong to an earlier incarnation.

I told Jan that I only admired Shimek for his intellect and taste in books. As soon as I said this, I realized by Jan's face that it was the wrong thing to say.

"He's dead," Jan said.

For a moment my mind closed, threw out all images, left me lost in a mental miasma. I was chilled to the bone, and the only thing that popped into my mind was the need to put on a sweater, my mother's lost sweater.

Shimek's father had trusted the promise of sanctuary that his German boss swore would be honored. Jan said that the German protector had been arrested for helping Jews and taken to Gestapo headquarters in Czortkow. (Later, rumor had it that he was sent to the front, but he was too old to be a soldier and we never learned what became of him.)

When the Gestapo arrested their protector and came to take Mr. Bosek to Czortkow, Shimek and his mother had somehow managed to slip out of the room. They made it as far as the greenhouse. "Their brains were splattered all over the glass," Jan reported.

In his letter, Shimek had written about a point that had recently occurred to him concerning the tale of the Grand Inquisitor in *The Brothers Karamazov*. He said he intended to join a partisan band if he made it to the forest.

Chapter Forty-six

WHILE AT HER PARENTS' HOUSE, Marynka had managed to obtain a warm jacket that her brother had peeled from a Jewish woman before taking her away to be killed. Marynka's taunting of Sidor with the jacket—saying how she had to look out for herself since she got no benefit from "his" Jews—drove him into a frenzy, and he smacked her across the face.

"Find out where they buried their gold," she said, "or I'll earn myself a pair of new boots." It was common knowledge that the Germans paid in boots for Jews turned in. She looked at us as if to say: See what I get for feeding you and carrying out your slop. (Actually my mother and I performed whatever tasks we could, but we couldn't go outdoors to get rid of waste.)

Over the weeks and months, Marynka's recriminations increased, particularly against my mother, who, it was true, barely concealed her contempt for "that dirty hussy, that murderer." Anyone who threatened to denounce human beings for a pair of boots or some scented soap deserved to be called "murderer," according to my mother.

My father received more courtesy from Marynka; in fact, when Jan wasn't around, she flirted with him, and my father's suave responses concealed the distaste it cost him. Marynka, vain about her small feet, would wiggle her toes along his leg, and he would promise her a pair of red boots from Paris as soon as the war was over. Not enough food to eat, yet talk of fancy boots didn't seem ludicrous at the time; to us it made perfect sense.

During Sidor and Marynka's fights, when Marynka threw the nearest shoe or broom and it clattered against the wall, Hania would come up to the attic to sit with us. Arthur slid over to give her a place near him. None of us said a word.

I could hear Sidor banging a fist tattoo on the table. "He's a good man," he said, speaking of my father. "I saw how he treated the men who worked for him on the bridge. I can't send him to his grave."

"Yes. Instead, you're digging your own and mine and Hania's. They'll shoot us in our own yard!"

"I'm the boss here. I know what I'm doing."

"You're a miserable dirty *Polack*," Marynka shouted as something heavy, probably a pail or a kettle, hit the wall, and since my back was leaning against its attic section, I felt the message come through my body and lodge like a rock under my ribs.

Every time Marynka and Sidor had one of their periodic fights, she would threaten that she was going to denounce him for hiding Jews, and at the end of the fight she would say that we had to leave, and Sidor would say no. My father would go down on his knees, kiss her hands and feet, and say, "You want the two of us to go, we'll go, but keep my children."

After the fight was over, it was quiet and the atmosphere would throb with fits and spurts of animosity and amiability. Then, a few days later, the drama would start all over again. The fights made us tremble—we feared we would eventually pay the price.

It was not Sidor and Marynka's screaming and yelling but some ruckus between my parents that traveled out the attic window and brought the inquisitive bachelor neighbor for another surprise visit. My father had continued to try to dissuade my mother from schemes such as bartering my hair—which Marynka coveted—to obtain a bath or selling her gold filling for food. He said that if we were meant to die of dirt and hunger, one bath or one ham wouldn't prevent it. Neither of the combatants won.

How Sidor and Marynka got rid of the neighbor they did not say. But from then on, our beds were clumps of hay in the barn between the wheezing horse and the cow that had stopped giving milk. To protect us from the intense night cold, Jan arrived in his horsedrawn wagon and unloaded a box that contained a down quilt and two blankets my parents had given him for safekeeping before they went to the ghetto (along with the suitcase of my mother's fancy clothes, found by his sister). One blanket my mother gave to Sidor in return for permission to cook something.

That night Sidor came to the barn and led her into the house. When he brought her back to the barn before dawn, she was carrying a pot of corn soup. "You thoughtless woman," my father muttered as he spooned the soup. A few times after that, she sneaked into the house when Sidor, Marynka, and Hania were working in the fields and came back with a few pancakes or a little gruel. "The smoke," my father said, "the neighbors can see it."

"We have to eat," she said.

The barn had no window. Through chinks in the vertical planks I surveyed the courtyard—the domain of half a dozen chickens, forlorn creatures dispirited by the absence of a rooster. Peeking into the yard when it rained, I could see the ruts in the ground fill up with little lakes that splashed Sidor or Marynka's legs when either of them ventured out with a dish of scraps or to empty our slop pails. At least in the barn I was spared Marynka's raucous voice, whether in argument or some rough jest. Sidor's face I missed: something benign that came through the eyes when he looked at me.

Arthur grew listless now that Hania no longer came to sit near him. At first, Arthur and Hania had ignored each other, but once in a while they'd make up a game. One of Hania's stockings rolled into a sphere became a ball, which they rolled back and forth to each other as they sat on the floor without speaking a word, their faces blank. Later they had taken to playing furious games in which the rules changed constantly. Now that was over, too, and Arthur became depressed.

The incarcerated feeling of my first few days at Sidor's, when I had felt the urge to run across the meadows, was gone; now I wanted to remain here, entrenched alongside the horse and cow, carried as they were in the diurnal pace of the creature world. The manure smell, strong as it was, didn't bother me after the first few hours. The barn at least had pacing room for my father. We made a hay nook for ourselves with bales and blankets for sleeping, but during the day we spread out to different corners. Arthur liked to sit near the horse, and I favored the cow.

Sidor's report that the Allies had landed in Sicily, and a few days later his specific mention of fighting in Salerno, letting the sound of the word roll off his tongue several times, brought free-floating excitement. Dare I let myself feel good, I wondered. The Germans might push them back into the sea. Still, the news gave me a twinge of gladness whenever it came to mind.

My father and Jan built a hiding place in the barn "for an emergency, for a few hours, maybe even a day." The hideout was in the miniature chicken coop that was attached, like a malignant growth, to the exterior wall of the barn. The cow's feeding trough, filled with hay and straw, stood against the barn's interior wall, behind which was the coop. Crawling between the legs on which the trough stood, my father made a hole in the barn wall into the coop. Then he made a very weak false wall of logs on the other side of the coop to separate us from the chickens, who were on shelves at the other end.

The space we stole from the chickens was the size of a closet. Wide enough for two people, it made a tight squeeze for four. The roof was too low for an adult to stand upright in it, and there was not enough room even to lie down. The angle of the roof pitch took getting used to, and at first only Arthur managed not to get numerous bumps on the head. We had to sit on the ground in a crouched position against one of the walls.

In our rehearsals, which my father insisted on to cut down our entry time into the coop, we always squirmed snakelike on our bellies through the hole in the barn wall in the same order:

first Arthur, then my mother, then me, then my father, who pulled in the brick over it. Sitting on straw in the barn after our latest trial run, we realized it took the four of us much too long to slither in and for my father to drag the plug into place.

Chapter Forty-seven

E ARLY ONE MORNING, not fully awake in the barn's gloom, I heard my father telling my mother his dream. It predicted that today was a special day, he didn't know in what way except that in the end we would be all right. I trusted my father's instincts for danger. He had known when to leave the ghetto and the Sternbergs' home, and he would know when to take us away from here, too.

Suddenly, I heard Rex barking, which is what he always did when strangers were approaching. I trusted Rex even more than my father. I peered through a chink in the barn wall: Gestapo men were jumping out of cars and motorcycles. Ukrainian militiamen were waving their rifles.

Rex's barking saved us, giving us a few precious seconds to scurry into the hiding place. My father had barely pulled in his legs after mine before I, lying on the floor, saw boots passing back and forth in front of the hole in the barn wall. There was no camouflage over it; my father hadn't had time to pull in the brick plug.

Clank and bang of heavy implements, grind of rusty hinges, swish and clomp of the cow and horse being prodded out of the barn. "Cursed dirty Jews," rang out when the slop pails spilled over polished boots. "Where are those damned Jews?" a voice bellowed in German a few inches beyond the wall. He shouted orders to the Ukrainians to search every corner of the barn.

They were looking specifically for Benjamin Gottesfeld and his wife and two children. Our blanket and down quilt, which they'd found in the barn, gave evidence that we'd been there. I waited to hear Marynka and Sidor's voices. They would be tortured to betray our hiding place.

My mother put her hand over Arthur's mouth. It wasn't necessary. We were too stunned to move or make a voluntary sound. My mother's chattering teeth split the silence for a few seconds until she managed to clamp her jaw together. My father dug some old throat lozenges out of his pocket and popped one in each of our mouths. The paper wrapper tearing sounded as loud as a rock-slide.

The Germans ordered the Ukrainians to dig holes in every part of the barn in the belief that we had a hiding place under the ground or had dug a tunnel that led under the river to the forest.

As they dug, pitchforkfuls of straw and dirt piled up in front of the uncovered hole in the barn wall. They were sealing us in and covering our hideout without realizing it. We had barely enough air to breathe.

The Germans, increasingly maddened by each hole that did not lead to our hiding place or supposed escape tunnel, threatened the Ukrainians with severe consequences if we were not found.

"Come out, Jews," a militiaman called out in Ukrainian, "we'll wrap you in white linen." He was referring to the shroud used for burial.

I heard our bachelor neighbor's familiar laugh and knew that it was he who had betrayed us. I heard other people laughing, screaming, cheering the diggers on. There seemed to be a large crowd in the barn, making a holiday out of waiting for us to be pulled out of hiding and shot.

Only a matter of minutes, I said to myself, any second now. It will be quick, right in the courtyard, up against the wall. A quick bullet to the brain would be merciful; I knew that. If I can just last through those few seconds. So often had I imagined my last moments that now, when the guns were only a foot away, I felt a queer numbness.

Then I thought of Dr. Steuerman's lover and what the Ukrainians had done to her body. They would shame me as a Jewish whore. Just as being Jan's girlfriend had protected me up until now, it would cause my body to be defiled after my death. Jan would not be able to prevent my shame.

Tears and saliva flowed from me; all my sphincters opened; nothing was left inside but the faint palpitation of waiting.

We soiled ourselves and each other over and over again.

The sound of spades digging first in one corner of the barn floor then in another continued for hours. We lost track of the time until we heard the chickens squawking. No one had come to feed them. The Germans and the militia were still there at night. Off and on I'd hear a spade hit a rock—and then curses.

It was quiet the next morning.

Late in the afternoon of that day, we heard Sidor's quavering voice. "Are you here?" he called over and over again. Obviously, the Germans had come back and were forcing him to act as a decoy. We didn't answer; we weren't going to fall into a trap. Then Sidor said, "I swear I'm alone. They're gone. Come out. You can come out now." But we couldn't. Finally, he realized that he had to dig the straw and muck away from the hole in the wall.

We crawled out of the coop, filthy and stinking. Sidor hugged each of us in turn, and we all cried, sometimes falling against each other. Sidor kept crossing himself, saying over and over that he had expected to find we had been killed.

For a moment I caught sight of Arthur standing alone, almost upright, yet sagging a little to one side. He stood on the spot like a stalk of corn in a field after the harvest, alive at the base only, deserted despite our being near him, neither awake nor asleep, blinking in the light, whimpering like the rest of us.

My mother, Arthur, and I sank down on a pile of hay in the barn while my father started to hobble about in an effort to get his legs operating again. Sidor, picking his way around the holes in the ground, left and came back with water for us. The cow and horse were gone.

Sidor told us that he and Marynka and Hania had been in the fields when the Germans had come looking for us. The Gestapo was waiting in the barn for them to return, but when they were on their way home from the fields, someone had told them what was happening. They had hidden in a neighboring village that night and most of the next day. They were warned, too, that the Germans had announced to the peasants that they were going to come back.

Sidor returned to the house and I expected to hear Marynka ranting.

Silence.

Chapter Forty-eight

A FEW HOURS AFTER DARK, Sidor returned to the barn and held out a loaf of bread. A whole loaf. None of us reached for it. Finally he put it in my mother's hands.

"You have to go," he said, looking at all of us.

For a second I thought, Give back the bread. But of course it wasn't a bribe.

"You have to go. They're coming back within twenty-four hours. They left a message."

Every second brought the Gestapo closer and yet we didn't move. To my mind there was only one place to go: back into the hiding place.

My father sank to his knees. "Have pity on my children," he begged. "Don't make them go." Sidor's face, a mask of stone, was new to me. My father told him again that after the war there would be no end to the rewards for him and his family. Clothes. Money. House. They would be members of our family as long as they lived.

Sidor went into the house again. He came back with the blanket we had given him and cut it into four parts.

"It's cold in the forest," he said. "I'll take you there."

A few rags from the blanket the raiders had torn during the

razzia lay about in the barn debris. I picked them up and stuffed them into my blouse while my mother foraged for anything that might have remained in one piece under the straw. She found the handle of a knife, turned it several times, then gave it to Arthur. We retied the rags around our feet. We no longer had shoes—the bad shoes we had worn when we first walked to Sidor's had long since fallen apart, and their disintegrated remains had blended into the straw of the barn.

At the courtyard gate, while Sidor scouted a bit in each direction, I turned around and saw a figure at the window. Marynka. She had her wish now. For a moment I wondered if she had earned a pair of boots for herself. May her legs break off if she did, I thought. But even though my mother had said that Marynka was capable of murder, I was sure she hadn't denounced us. She must be furious with Sidor. He'd be killed if he was found with us. But he had won over her once again.

That march to the forest, first round and about through back roads out of the village, and then through fields and ditches and quagmires and along the river, my feet lifting themselves into the path trod by my mother ahead of me, seemed longer than any three hours of night I'd ever lived through. Once in a while we stopped, so that whoever was carrying Arthur, Sidor or my father, could shift him to the other one's shoulders.

It was still pitch-dark when we came to the first line of trees. Sidor lifted Arthur off his shoulders. "I'm going," he said but stood still. He started to say "May God . . ." A crackle in the underbrush drove him away.

My father put Arthur on his shoulders and took my mother's hand. "Wait," she said and broke off a piece of bread for each of us. We ate as we walked straight ahead. Walking into the forest was just as terrifying as walking into the ocean—which I knew about from books—in the way it swallows you up. We were walking away from the killers at our rear and toward their victims ahead. Let's stop right here, I wanted to say to my father, but it was too much of an effort to speak.

Picking our way between pine trees, we came to a sudden clearing. Before we could duck out of the moonlit gap, a figure approached. A scout for hidden Jews, he had been tracking us but, fearing we might be decoys, had waited until the moon revealed my father's face.

He led us to an enclave of earthen dugouts—some protruding into contoured rises, some level with the forest floor—all camouflaged with branches and leaves. About 150 Jews from Skala and *shtetls* in the area had fled to the forest one or two at a time after the *aktsia* and after the liquidation of the Borszczow ghetto, and these bunkers were their last shelter.

"He's here, Benjamin Gottesfeld is here," passed along their grapevine. I knew my father was held in high esteem in our town, but these reverent whispers appointed him wizard, someone with a sixth sense who knew how to escape the enemy beyond the trees. One of my father's old cronies came to lead him to a bunker where a group of men waited. "You're here. Now the war will end," I heard him say. My father was asked over and over for news about the Russian advance.

The Jews in the forest spent the daytime hours in their underground bunkers. After dark, some of the men and boys would come out, one by one, to beg or steal a little food from the peasants. This was dangerous; it was a matter of life and death to scrounge a little bit of food, and many of these volunteers never returned. The Jews were all starving; many had already died of hunger and exposure.

The Ukrainian peasants knew where the Jews were hiding. Individual peasants and German units had periodically invaded the forest to try to ferret them out, and some Jews had died in these dragnets. There had been warnings that a full-scale assault on the forest was planned and it was expected at any moment, my father's friends told him.

My father motioned us to a space under a tree and announced that we were not going to build a bunker; we were leaving as soon as it got dark. Staying in the forest, he said, would be our death.

My mother begged to stay just one more day. She had just found her brother Wolf and his wife and daughters, who had escaped to the forest from the Borszczow ghetto before its liquidation.

Uncle Wolf told my mother that he and his family were pariahs in the forest because of Grandfather Jakob's betrayal of the Jews in hiding to the Germans. Bitterly he complained that people didn't trust him. They said, If your father could do such a thing, so could you.

My mother still did not believe the story of what Jakob had done in the ghetto. She denied it as a Ukrainian lie, a slander that was unproved since no Jews who could have witnessed it had survived to verify the event. Until her dying day, my mother denied that the story was true.

Wolf begged her for bread for his children, but she said she didn't have any. "What should I do?" she asked my father. "Should I give him some?"

"Am I Solomon?" my father asked, walking off to someone who had waved to him.

I wanted to stay, too. I had just found Lotka.

Chapter Forty-nine

Lotka crept up with soundless forest expertise, and bear-hugged me from the rear. I turned around and embraced her. Lotka was skeletally thin. Traces of the forest clung to her hair and her ragged clothes, and lodged under the nails of her swollen blue fingers. One foot had a makeshift bandage anchored to the remnants of a shoe. "Refused to make way for a burning log," she said, pointing to her foot. "Damn thing won't heal. You don't have a bit of ointment, do you?" I had nothing to give her and took care not to burden her with sympathy.

It was already light when she led me to the bunker she shared with Rubcio—big, husky Rubcio, whom I'd once had a crush on.

It took months, Lotka said, to become familiar with the forest and learn how to build bunkers and cover them with earth in which young trees were planted. I had probably walked over the heads of dozens of people without knowing it.

The bunkers were of different sizes, depending on how many people—two, three, six—were living in them. Every few weeks, people moved to another part of the forest if they felt the Ukrainian peasants were becoming too aware of their presence.

Whenever she and Rubcio could scratch a bit of cornmeal from an abandoned sack they picked wild mushrooms, made a fire deep in the forest, and cooked a little soup. They had no water except what could be saved from rain and dew. I asked about the smoke; surely people living near the forest would see it. "We take a chance very late at night," she said.

Lotka reversed the bandage on her leg and I saw the festering wound. "We work every moment," she said, then she blushed; perhaps she was thinking of stolen moments with Rubcio. I wanted to ask if her parents, who had forbidden an alliance with him in the old Skala days, knew about her and Rubcio, then realized it didn't matter.

No secrets here; in the next bunker a "high-born" girl lived with a former water-carrier. A woman from one of Skala's finest families, who had lost her husband and child, was now living with the town's only Jewish thief. My father was devastated when he learned that girls from the best families were living with old men who had lost everybody and everything.

"Why not?" asked Lotka. "We'll soon be gone anyway."

Lotka told me that her parents no longer lived in the house we had once shared with them; they slept where Mottel worked—in Gestapo headquarters. Holdouts to the last in Skala, the Sternbergs still counted on their Gestapo angel for protection.

"It's crazy," I said.

"I know." She thrust her hand under her flimsy jacket and drew something out on her fingernail. She laughed as she squashed a louse and dug in for another one. "I prefer to associate with these vermin rather than with the ones they rely on."

We sat there for hours catching up. I told her about Jan and me and the asylum my family and I had found at Sidor's and about the *razzia* there a few days before. After we sat in silence for a moment, choked by private agonies and common terror, Lotka began to talk of the forest itself, how it kept her going: birdsong in the trees, the ingenuity of nature evident in a morning mushroom, the forest's silence as a presence that soothes and cleanses the spirit.

"Rubcio and I tried to join a Russian partisan group, but they wouldn't take us," Lotka told me. Only one man had succeeded in joining one of the four partisan units that passed through this part of the forest.

"We're starting a Jewish group," Rubcio said. "Will you join us?" Lotka added, "Anyone can shoot a gun."

"Yes, but first we have to have one in hand," I said. So far they had nothing: no arms, no leader, no military knowhow. "I'll think about it," I said, knowing I was stalling. I admired their dream of wanting to go down fighting, but I couldn't desert my parents and my brother, and my father and Jan would never let me leave them.

I walked a crisscross path back to my parents, passing people sitting at the entrances of bunkers. Some, too weak to manage more of a greeting than a fleeting nod of the head, sat immobile, hoarding air in their lungs before another suffocating night underground. Some turned over bits of clothing in the hunt for lice. Others lay on the ground in an agony of high fever. Typhus. "Water," a little girl moaned as I passed, "a little water."

A woman I knew who used to live on the next street had a baby at her breast. "There's nothing," she said, "but I let him suck."

This was not the only baby born in the forest. One woman who had grown children and whose period had stopped before she escaped to the forest had given birth to a girl. Her husband had bit off the umbilical cord. Then he took the baby and left her on the steps of a nunnery. Later, they learned that by the time the nuns found the baby and took her inside, she was dead. I shuddered when I heard the story, thinking what would happen with my baby if I got pregnant.

My mother gestured for me to follow her behind a few low-growing trees and then gave me my share of bread. Arthur sat next to my father, chewing his mouthful slowly, which enraged my mother. "Hurry," she said. "Someone will see."

My father returned the rest of his portion to her. "For Wolf's children," he said. It meant that his ulcerated stomach hurt too much for him to eat.

He had seen Lolla—we had all seen her and her two sons. They were living in a crude dugout. Lolla was totally bald and had a deep, deep scar on her head from the knife the peasants had plunged into her brain. She and the two boys were starving.

Lolla wanted my father to build a shelter large enough for us and for her and her children. My mother pleaded with him to do so. "If we go and leave them, we're leaving them to die," she said.

My father refused. "Staying here is our death," he repeated. Jews who banded together, he had learned in the ghetto, invited their own destruction.

But where to go?

My mother did not give my father's portion of bread to Wolf's children but kept it for us. Retying the rags around Arthur's feet, she told him to hurry up with his bread, but his jaws rose and fell at the slow pace of a bird's wings wafting through the sky in glide after glide.

"We have to get a message to Jan," my father said. I offered to go as soon as it got dark. No, he said, we would wait a day for him to find us, and if he didn't, then I could go.

I decided to join Lotka and Rubcio's band after I had made sure that Jan would lead my parents and Arthur out of the forest.

I spent the rest of the day with Lotka and Rubcio. He spoke of plans to acquire guns and ammunition, and promised to teach me how to shoot. His hand rested on Lotka's knee as she sat cross-legged beside him. Jan and I never held hands when anyone else was present. Each stolen coming together was accompanied in my head by the refrain: "the last time." The last time together, the last time to make love—that thought must have been with Lotka and Rubcio, too, but Lotka's hand, as she placed it on Rubcio's thigh, signaled a serenity that Jan and I had never known.

Rubcio walked me back to the tree that would shelter our family for one more night. For him, the lack of a gun was harder to bear than hunger, icy nights, and lice. The night the Germans and Ukrainians had come through with fixed bayonets, the only weapon he had was a paring knife, but they had passed over his bunker.

"Talk to Jan," he said. "Convince him to be a courier for us." I promised I would enlist Jan as a gunrunner.

Chapter Fifty

WE SPENT THE NIGHT sleeping under a tree, planning to leave the forest when it got light and we could see our way.

Shots and screams woke me. On my pine-needle bed, I felt the pounding of feet even before my eyes could make out figures running in all directions in the predawn darkness.

Gunfire and explosions erupted ahead of and behind us, and bullets whizzed past our heads. "Keep down," I screamed as my father and mother shielded Arthur between them.

Smelling smoke from bunkers hit by grenades, hearing the screams of people trapped inside, I got to my knees before my father pulled my ankle and I fell flat again.

The Ukrainians dropped piles of smoking and burning straw into the remaining bunkers to roast and asphyxiate anyone who did not crawl out.

German and Ukrainian voices yelling orders mixed with the screams of people wounded or on fire, and the human sounds, mixing with the shooting and explosions, became louder, then ebbed and became louder once again.

End of the line. Nowhere to run. No hole in the ground to crawl into. At least I'd be spared the humiliation of my dead body that I had expected during the *razzia* at Sidor's.

"Let it be quick," kept repeating itself in my head.

Paralysis set in. I was sure I wouldn't be able to get up when the moment came. They'd have to shoot me lying down. Ages and ages, an endless time-block, held me limbless, a useless thing, so that when I finally died, there wouldn't be much to kill anymore. Fright itself became minimal, and barely kept me ticking in a low throb all that day.

By evening, when it was quiet at last, most of the Jews in the forest were dead.

Somehow, miraculously, we four had survived the bullets, the grenades, the fire, the smoke.

Morning.

The shadow of a pair of boots fell across my face.

Jan.

It seemed natural for him to be here. Without knowing it, I had been expecting him.

After he saw my eyes blink, he walked around to my father and mother and Arthur. They weren't hurt. I was sure I had been shot in the back, just like the time when I had run through Grandfather Jakob's lumber yard during the *aktsia* in Skala. Jan examined every inch of my body but could find no bullet or bleeding. None of us could believe we were alive.

Jan told us that when a militiaman, after the *razzia* at Sidor's, claimed that "the Gottesfelds escaped to Russia," he went to check with Sidor. Sidor told him we were in the forest.

"I had to wait till it was over." He gave me a sip of water from a tin canister, then held my face in his hands as if my cheeks were the petals of a rare flower he'd never seen before.

He told my father he would sneak me into the hiding place in the attic of his barn and come back for Arthur. Then on the third trip he would come back for them. "It may not be until tomorrow," he said.

Walking close behind Jan, I heard what sounded like a branch snapping, but then the sound clearly became that of footsteps. "Run!" shouted Jan.

Turning around, I saw a big guy two years my senior who had

always wound up in the same class with me in Polish elementary school because he'd been left back. But in the forest he had become a leader.

He was chasing Jan and me; perhaps he was afraid Jan was going to betray the few Jews left alive after the massacre. But in that moment, when he was pursuing us, we didn't know what he wanted—to kill Jan or force him to do something or to stop us from leaving.

I ran as fast as I could and managed to keep Jan in sight as he skittered to the side, then doubled back and jumped over a gully. Every time I turned around, he, brandishing a stick, was still coming after us. Finally, at the end of the forest, he lost us.

Chapter Fifty-one

IN HIS BARN THAT EVENING, Jan leaned the ladder in place, and I followed him up into the hideout I'd left in what seemed to be several lives ago. Jan held me in his arms for a while, but I could not release the dam of tears that were ready to burst. "Go get Arthur," I said.

He sat down near the window opening and I went over to sit by him as I had done so many times before. "Please," I said. He had just risked his life by going to the forest, and now I was sending him back into the jaws of death.

He bent down for a kiss and I received it but could not return one of my own. I saw my father and mother and Arthur lying side by side on the pine needles. The raiders might come back, they usually did. "Go—now." He got up and disappeared down the ladder without a word.

When Jan handed Arthur to me at the top of the ladder, I was gripped by a quick scare. I thought Arthur had been wounded after all. Even the dreamy, beingless blob he had learned to become when a cough or a sneeze could give us away, even the inanimate, thin little figure clinging to my mother's lap or my father's shoulder or Jan's back, had now lost the apparent vestiges of life-tension. He just lay on the straw. I kissed him, rubbed his hands and feet, held him and rocked him, and finally, as if after a deep sleep, he opened his eyes. "He won't come back," he said.

"Who? Papa?"

"No, Jan. I heard your friend say he almost caught him as he ran out of the forest with you and that he would trap him the next time."

I gave Arthur a drink of water from Jan's canister. "Well, he didn't succeed. Jan brought you, didn't he?"

"Yeah, but that was because there was shooting somewhere and we ducked past it. They're going to kill him. I heard them say it. He's a murderer like the others. They're going to do it."

"Stop it," I said. Maybe it was better to have a somnolent creature than this doomsayer. I glared at him.

"You'll see." He turned to the wall with an emphatic twist, as if for the rest of his life.

The following night, after Jan's third trip to the forest, when my parents and Arthur were lying on their straw bed and Jan and I had settled down together, I asked him if he knew what had happened to Lotka and Rubcio.

He told me that the Germans had captured them. Rubcio, together with his mother and sister and other Jews, had been taken to another place in the forest and shot.

There was no longer any need to ask Jan to become a gunrunner for Rubcio and his fighting band.

Lotka's father had managed, through his Gestapo boss, to save his daughter from being shot in the forest. Somehow he had brought her to where he and his wife were living—Gestapo headquarters.

From our hiding place in the barn's attic, we couldn't see Jan's neighbors as they came into the yard, but we heard them greeting each other. A voice screeched, "The forest is cleaned out. No more pigs." Jan's mother shouted, "Finally got their due," and his sister added, "About time." A list of dead Jews was recited and amended: "So-and-so's family but not the son," and then, "No, they got the son too."

"Gottesfeld's Benjamin, did they get the swine yet?" someone asked. Jan's mother answered with authority, since they were known as her son's Jews: "They ran to Russia. We'll get them when they come back."

"They got the wife's brother, you know, Wasserman's Wolf, the one with the egg warehouse." Jan's sister added, "Yeah, the whole family." Wolf and his wife and children had been killed by a grenade thrown into their bunker. Lolla and her sons had perished the same way.

My mother stepped back and rapped her fist slowly like a dirge on her heart. "He asked me for a little bread for the children." Barely forcing the words out, she kept saying over and over, "for the children, for the children."

"What good would it have done?" my father whispered. Nothing he or I said could distract her from obsessing over her sin, as she called it. Her grief jelled into despair over the creature she had become, an animal just like the wolf, the direct opposite of her good-natured brother. She wrapped her arms around her head. "A wolf can at least howl," she said.

Down in the yard, the neighbors laughed and jeered about how uppity the Jews used to be, how they'd believed they knew more than peasants. "What they knew was how to finagle what they wanted out of us." The group must have closed ranks because their voices died down and smothered under a burst of hilarity. Then we heard them talking about the immorality in the forest, how couples had paired in random combinations. "They all screwed in the open, like animals."

"And she was pregnant," I heard someone say. "Her father thought he was a big shot, that his boss would save her." A sick feeling hit me. They were talking about Lotka. A man reported that after Lotka was reunited with her parents, the Germans had lured away Mottel's Gestapo boss and gone in and shot the three of them in their beds. "Too good for them," Jan's mother said. "I would have known what to do with the sinners."

I couldn't bear to think of Lotka lying in a pool of blood. "How often did I tell Mottel not to wait any longer?" my father said. "Stupid," my mother said, "to let herself get pregnant."

That night Jan brought me a note from Lotka:

I have a feeling I will join Rubcio soon. I did want to live long enough to have the baby. Now I think, what for? It was wonderful to see you in the forest. Remember me as your good friend and cousin,

Lotka

Later, I asked Jan why he had kept Lotka's death a secret from me. "I was waiting for the right moment," he said.

I turned on him. "What right moment?" My throat seemed to be lined with sandpaper.

"You're always mad at me when there's bad news." His voice was no smoother than mine. "I can't save the whole world."

Chapter Fifty-two

FOR THE NEXT TWO WEEKS, Jan traveled from town to village, from house to house, trying to find someone to hide us. Anyone he approached could have denounced him on the spot. A Polish saddler spat at him, saying, "You're as bad as a Jew," spitting "Jew" at him as the curse word it was for the Poles. Among Ukrainians, only one agreed to have us for a few hours, or at most overnight, as a personal favor to Jan. My father said to forget about four slots, but to find a place for Arthur and me. When my mother heard this her face contorted for a scream, but no sound came out. After a minute she gasped a few times and said, "No. Arthur stays with me."

Every morning I thought, This is the day we'll go to the Gestapo. A host with time-bomb guests on his threshold, Jan had every right to slam the door in our faces. "Something will turn up," he would say when all he could find to bring us were a few potatoes or a jug of water. I understood that he'd protected us for so long that our lives no longer belonged to us, they belonged to him, too. For the rest of his life he'd hear the door as it slammed shut in his face.

One morning, during the special quiet that meant it was Sunday, I heard Jan enter the barn. After his usual clothes-changing interval, he appeared in the attic in his knockabout clothes, holding a small red zinnia. He plopped down on a hay pillow with a sigh of relief and rubbed his neck.

Skipping church didn't save him from wearing a stiff collar; it was part of his courting outfit. His mother had begun accusing him of hiding me somewhere since he showed no interest in finding a wife. So the charade of finding a new girlfriend had begun again. Every time he took off to search out a hiding place for us, his family thought he was chasing girls.

"They're all the same," he said. "Blond, blue-eyed, and round-bottomed." No one could accuse me of those things, especially not of roundness. My skirt, once tailored to fit, hung down like a curtain that had an empty room behind it.

Jan took me down to the barn to let me exercise my legs. He sat in a far corner, watching me tramp from trough to horse stall, up and down; and the more he looked at me, the harder I marched about. Finally I gave in and went to him, to the half-circle of his seated body waiting ready to receive me. His desire sparked mine, and even though it was foolhardy, we made love. Last time, last time. And that thought gave way to: They haven't got me yet, not yet.

After we climbed up the ladder again, my father and mother awoke from a nap. Arthur, hovering near the window, said, "A man's coming."

Jan sprinted downstairs before the visitor could knock. It was Sidor. I heard him ask if we were here.

He had come to take us back, he said, sitting down on the straw. Italy had capitulated, he explained, and he trusted my father's assertion, made months earlier, that the fall of Italy would be the sign that Germany would lose the war. My father nodded: the Germans were too smart to commit suicide, Napoleon-style, in Russia. The war would end before winter.

With just a quick trace of his old beaming smile, Sidor assured us that it would be safe to come back. Marynka had agreed with him that now no one would dream we were hiding there.

"I was afraid you were killed in the forest," Sidor said.

We returned to Sidor's that night. It was bitterly cold outside and indoors, and we were freezing and exhausted. All seven of us slept in the kitchen on their one bed. We slept horizontally with our feet resting on a bench from the alcove that Sidor put alongside the bed.

The next morning, Sidor shoved a ripped and almost feather-less quilt in after us before he closed the entry hole of the hiding place in the chicken coop. No more spending time spread out in the barn, and no more leaving the brick cover for my father to pull shut from the inside. Sidor sealed us in.

When I crawled inside, I couldn't imagine how I'd get through the next day. Braided like a horse's tail, we had spent a maximum of two full days in there during the raid. Now, coming out for five minutes would be the longed-for exception.

When bright daylight forced strips of illumination through the cracks in the coop, I cherished each bit of wall or cloth that changed from black or gray into tones of color.

Sidor had spread fresh straw in the coop, but it was still the same tight fit. We sat crunched against the wall, unable to lie down, and when one of us turned, the other three had to turn as well. Sometimes Arthur had to sit on my father's lap. We twisted and moved to avoid the rats scurrying through the coop; some-times they bit us.

Even in September the temperature went below freezing at night. No matter how much I curled and uncurled my fingers and toes, my hands and feet felt numb, but my body sweated from being pressed against three others. The person on each end always pulled Sidor's old quilt to cover the icy edges, but the ones in the middle wanted it off.

Sometimes Marynka or Sidor came by to bring stewed potato peels or other scraps, but some days neither one came and our chamber pot wasn't emptied. Often it spilled as we changed places to use it.

The ravenous relatives of the lice Lotka had killed so expertly between her fingers in the forest crawled through our clothes and hair and fed on us with gusto.

All day and night we killed the lice on our bodies, but the more we killed, the more of them attacked us. Since it was too dark to see them even during the day, we relied on touch. For my mother, the champ delouser, this became a full-time occupation.

There were so many lice that my hair was moving.

Chapter Fifty-three

ONE DAY MARYNKA came by with a small pot of beans and said that Sidor was very sick but she was afraid to call a doctor. Sidor, in his delirium, might speak our names. "Maybe I should call the priest."

"Same risk as a doctor," my father said.

"Not for his soul," she answered.

Sidor had typhus, apparently having contracted it from the infected lice we had brought back from the forest. Typhus kept him in bed for three weeks.

Not long after he recovered, my father and I fell into the daze of illness. Of those weeks I can only remember waking at moments to an agonizing thirst and then sinking again into a stupor. Both of us at different times, my mother later said, appeared to sink without rallying, and all she could do was pray. I pulled out of the coma before my father, then I lay despondent, convinced he would die. It was four weeks, according to my mother, who used her lips on our foreheads as a thermometer, before my father and I were fever-free.

My recuperation brought a consuming interest in what Sidor or Marynka would bring us to eat. Hunger I had thought of as a gnawing mouse in the stomach; now it became a rat that took up lodging in my body and chewed on my mind. All I wanted to talk about was food: wiener schnitzel with eggs and anchovies and fried potatoes. When the fever was replaced by consuming hunger, my mother gave me part of her and my father's portions, not knowing that each morsel goaded my appetite even more.

Often, in that hole, inhaling each other's breath as our only sustenance for twelve or thirty-six hours at a time, we fabricated dream menus: my mother reciting ingredients for recipes—"Take a nice fat carp"; my father reminiscing about dishes he had sampled in Czernowitz cafés; Arthur recalling his favorite jam or the orange he had been given for Chanukah.

As my mother became more and more silent, free of complaints and criticism, a being who conserved every iota of energy to keep her inner pilot light lit, so my father became more expansive, reciting Goethe or Schiller or Shakespeare's soliloquies. At times his mood required prose, and Arthur and I would listen to partly paraphrased but nonetheless extensive portions of novels by Polish and Yiddish writers.

When no literary urge seized my father, he'd try to boost our spirits by speaking of what would happen after the war. Paris, of course, and lots to eat and pretty clothes; for me, medical school, and for Arthur, what? Stuck on what Paris had to offer Arthur, he'd find a panorama to view: Paris from the top of the Eiffel Tower or from the steps of the Sacré Coeur, and Arthur had to remind him that great heights made him dizzy.

My father began to reminisce about long ago. He'd offer bits of family lore to cheer us up. He spoke of his father, Grandfather Azriel—whose portrait as a young man with a flower in his tunic I'd often seen in the family album—as a military man with a distinguished record and a medal to prove it. My father's voice wavered with habitual admiration without any note that the Austro-Hungarian Empire was a bit of whipped cream that had soured long ago. Grandfather Azriel, lost in Belzec, did not exist; in his place my father gave us the debonair soldier executing a smart salute for his emperor.

Chapter Fifty-four

CHRISTMAS EVE, 1943. After midnight, Sidor invited us into the house. He picked Arthur up since his legs refused to carry him. In the shuttered house, the room's single candle seared my eyes. A bottle of vodka stood center stage on the table. Sidor took a swig as he carried a large pail to the fire on the stove, and Marynka donated the last kettleful of heated water.

I cried as I washed my face, hands, and chest for the first time in many months. My mother unbuttoned Arthur's shirt and scrubbed him with a heel of brown soap, then stripped to the waist and washed her face, neck, arms, and chest. When she finished toweling Arthur and herself with a bedsheet, I asked Hania to hold it as a screen, which she did conscientiously. Since she wasn't very tall, Sidor and Marynka were still afforded a full view of my body, but I didn't care.

Hania said she wished I'd come live in the house again, then she wouldn't be so afraid. "Afraid of what?" I asked, thinking she meant her mother. I'd often seen Marynka smack the girl across the face and head without warning.

"The Germans are coming to shoot me and burn down the house," she said. "And they're going to kill Rex, too." I asked her how she knew that. "My mother said it would happen when they came for you."

My impulse was to deny what her mother had told her. She stood there, still very much a child, her eyes solemn, clearly not asking me for a counter-story. There was something she wanted to ask but had difficulty finding the words. She had seen cows and pigs and chickens slaughtered, but a bullet made such a small hole.

"Does it hurt while the blood is coming out?" I put my arms around her and said, "No, no, it all goes very fast. Besides, they don't want you." I told her not to think about such things; it was Christmas, I said, and next Christmas I would have a present for her.

Marynka washed my hair with kerosene to kill the lice. "Take it," I said, when she said she wished my hair was hers. What would she do with a mass of black hair? Certainly not use it for a wig; even if someone could be found to make it for her, it would have to be dyed. Only blond hair was considered beautiful. Maybe she wants it, I thought, to stuff a pillow.

After a few more drinks of vodka, she started on my breast, how round and firm they were; hers, she complained, were no more than pimples, even when she was pregnant. Here I was, all skin and bones, and Marynka was jealous because she was flat-chested. There was nothing I could say. Instead of making her merry, the vodka had made her irritable. At any moment she might order us out of the house.

We sipped vodka from the common cup. When my turn came to make a toast, I thanked them for the bath, which they had guessed was my most fervent wish. When his turn came, my father toasted friendship; and when my mother stood up, she seemed to stand frozen by our stares. Even in the best of times she had never been much of a talker. Oh God, I thought, she's going to say something like "Cleanliness is next to godliness" while looking at Marynka.

Holding up the cup she said, "Let's drink to Sidor and his family. May they have a healthy Christmas, and let's hope the Russians get here soon, and"—she hesitated, looking at my father and me, and then said—"and that the ring of dirt we left on the pail isn't so deep that it can't be scrubbed off." We clapped and sipped, and for a moment I looked around in astonishment. This was the first time any of us had smiled in Sidor and Marynka's house.

The little alcove in the far wall, with its lumpy pillows, seemed to taunt me. I couldn't help thinking how the alcove had constricted every change of position when Jan used to join me there and yet I had thought of it as a bower of comfort. That had been before the *razzia* here and the *aktsia* in the forest, when food and water and a bit of heat from the stove came to us daily, when Jan visited at least once a week and my father still promised to take us all to Paris after the war. Paris, it occurred to me, might be as demolished as the Jewish enclave in the forest.

Hania took a stool and went to sit with Arthur. He ignored her. She offered him a worn-looking top—a toy Sidor must have made for Christmas years before—and a few walnuts her mother had hidden away since the harvest. Arthur took the walnuts. She demonstrated how the top worked, but he refused to look at its mesmerizing revolutions. He twirled each walnut in turn, but not one of them would spin.

Then Marynka mixed a basin of dough, put out some sugar Jan had brought, and fried so many pancakes that a batch was left on the table when Sidor led us out just before dawn with Arthur in his arms. Even Rex couldn't eat any more. We all had stomach aches that day. I cherished every twinge of pain.

Chapter Fifty-five

A BOUT TWICE A WEEK, Marynka uncovered the opening of the hideout, gestured to my father to come out, and then sealed us in again. Usually it was in the afternoon when she came home early from the fields or when Sidor went to a peasants fair. At first I assumed that she wanted my father to do a chore of some kind; but then she began to appear in the middle of the night.

I couldn't ask my mother what Marynka wanted him for because I had already guessed the answer and didn't want to hear it. Now that Jan wasn't around much to flirt with Marynka, she needed someone to listen to her fanciful speeches, or maybe she wanted to hear my father speak of city life. That's all they do, they talk, I kept saying to myself. If there's more, my father is a more resilient man than he looks. My father, mother, and I never said a word about these outings, and since no one spoke of them we could pretend they didn't happen.

Then Sidor came to get my mother. She looked at my father and he nodded. Had Sidor discovered Marynka's pranks and vowed to get even, I wondered. And how would he allow her to find out about his own excursions without severe consequences?

While my mother was gone, my father went into one of his recitations. On this day, he chose to recall his favorite biography, one on Napoleon; and Arthur and I, led by my father, observed Napoleon's triumph during his visit to a conquered city. The mystique of Napoleon-worship had gripped my father as long as I could remember, and in the hiding place the conquering emperor thrilled him more than ever. But each accolade Napoleon received diverted me less and less as I grew anxious over my mother's long absence. Eventually she crawled back in with a large hunk of bread in her hands, but my father remained imperturbable as he went on with the story.

Once in a while Sidor asked for my mother again, but not as often as Marynka came for my father. Once Arthur, addressing no one in particular, said, "No one ever asks *me* to come out."

This frenzy puzzled me: either they did very little or they had huge appetites. When Jan and I managed to sit down together, we spent most of our time just holding each other. Had Sidor and Marynka drunk aphrodisiacs? It didn't make sense that at this stage they would want to exercise their mastery over Jews like medieval seigneurs.

As the weeks melded into months, and the hardest months of winter permitted no variation other than the sound of a storm or the absence of it during a snowfall, our chances of remaining alive until the war was over seemed acutely remote.

Uberleben, the Yiddish word for "survival," spelled doubt for me. Survive another day—and then what? All I could imagine was a ruined world populated by creatures out of a painting by Bosch who would torture me with hells I had not yet experienced. To live—if that word could be used for what we were doing in our coop—to live *uber*, "over, beyond," our current existence, what did it mean: "over" in the sense of above it, disembodied, floating over everything as in a dream? Did it mean a challenge to prevail beyond physical endurance?

To live one more day would be a miracle. But I had to, I had to try my utmost to live another day. My mother, my father, and Arthur had no link to life without me.

Chapter Fifty-six

J AN HADN'T SEEN ME since my illness, but I knew by the way he looked at me that he was frightened by more than my emaciated state. I tottered on his arm as he led me around in the barn. My joints had ossified, at least it felt as if I had no joints at all, and I begged to sit.

His face was bruised and some dried blood stuck to the side of his mouth. A German patrol along the river had taken him for a smuggler, and when all they found on him was a sausage and some bread, they beat him and vowed to waylay him on his return. I told him that not knowing how much longer I had to hold out had become the severest trial. "I have to know when the Russians will come," I said.

"Ask me for medicine and I can go to the pharmacy. Maybe there's none to be had, but I know where to go for it. Where do you want me to go for predictions about the war? Should I ask a bird who flew over the lines?" The more he spoke, the more vehement he sounded. "Rumors there are plenty. You want rumors?"

Sidor couldn't buy a newspaper because everyone knew he couldn't read. Besides, the reports were doctored by the Germans to make it appear that they were winning the war when actually they were losing.

Even when Sidor remembered rumors about troop movements heard from other peasants or in the marketplace, and even when he got the geography right, the reports had been distorted by German lies and Ukrainian fears of Soviet conquest well before they filtered down to him. By this time the Ukrainians no longer trusted the Germans or believed they were going to give them an independent state, as they'd once hoped and expected, but they hated the Russians more than the Germans, and they hated the Jews more than both put together.

Sidor and Marynka's food deliveries to us fluctuated not only with how much they had but also with the rumors about the progress of the war. We knew the Russians had won a victory because they would bring us a little bowl of soup or something else. When Sidor heard that the Germans had withdrawn from the west bank of the Dnieper River, he came to celebrate with a small pot of kasha. We ate every grain as if it were a delicacy and begged him for more bulletins. But when they heard in the marketplace that the Germans were advancing, they didn't bring us anything to eat. Sometimes Sidor cursed the day he'd taken us back. Sidor was a sweet, decent guy, but he was also sick and tired of the risks of sheltering us, of the work it involved, of the fear, the suspicion, of the war itself.

Once Sidor called my father out into the barn to say he had lost belief in the prophecy that the war would end in the spring. He said he didn't believe in spring anymore; there was nothing to eat in the house, his child was starving, and he would have no seeds to plant even if he had the strength to plow the ground. Sidor admitted that the battles with Marynka had begun again and that she still had her eyes on a pair of red boots if he himself didn't drive us out.

Through the opening I saw my father fall to his knees in front of Sidor. "Please, for my children, don't push them to their death." I could see Sidor's shoes walking up and down past my father. "The war is ending," my father said. "We'll be like one big family."

"Talk," Sidor said, "just talk," and he motioned my father back into the hideout.

On one of his visits, Jan brought a letter from Aunt Sophia. She and Uncle Zygmunt and Dolek, still hiding in Wasil's attic, were close to despair. For seven days they'd had no bread. There were rumors of a *razzia*.

The Gestapo had come to search the house and found Wasil singing while working on his gate. "Why are you singing?"

"Why shouldn't I sing?" Wasil replied. "I have nothing to worry about. I am a poor man. I live alone. Go to the peasants who don't sing. They're rich from the Jews they hide in their houses. They worry. I sing." My aunt wrote that the Gestapo had left without entering the yard but with a promise to return.

She was keeping a diary, Aunt Sophia wrote, in which she inscribed many such stories. "Death is no longer fearful," she added. She prayed daily for Dolek to be saved.

My father instructed Jan to say they should hold on. "Tell her I said the war will end in a few weeks." His message, I realized, was meant to instill resolve in her, but betrayed, in the offhand way he spoke the words, that at that moment he didn't believe it himself. Though certain the Germans would soon be defeated, my father admitted that "soon," if it meant more than a week or two, would be too late. One "soon" miraculously followed another. No more "soon" is all I wanted.

I told Jan to find someone who listened to the news reports from the BBC. Hardly anyone had an illegal shortwave radio, and among the few who did, he said, "Who do you think will admit to a militiaman that he listens to forbidden broadcasts?"

He held me close, and his eight calloused fingers felt like salve on a wound as he stroked my cheeks. We were too exhausted to talk or move. "I'll be back," he said before he left.

Chapter Fifty-seven

WHEN SIDOR CAME to bring us some bread and muttered something about February coming to an end and "bringing an end to everything," I realized that Jan had not come by since sometime in January. Then one evening he arrived by horse and wagon with his friend Stasiek.

We had been in the same class, Stasiek and I—in fact he was the same Stasiek who had rolled up and pinned my hair back so the commissar teacher wouldn't pick on me. It was from Stasiek that Jan sometimes got food for us, which Stasiek had taken from his mother. Now Stasiek had consented to come in the wagon, since Jan had trouble getting past the patrols alone. He waited in the house with Sidor and Marynka.

Jan and I sat opposite each other in the barn on bales of hay, and he reached for my hand. I knew I stank to high heaven. So what. The news was bad, he said; the Russian offensive to liberate the Ukraine had stopped. He spoke in a monotone, as if he were talking about shoe leather: that's what had been delivered, take it or leave it, it was all the same to him. Shoes were on my mind since the rags around my feet were giving out. When the Russians came, I would have to try to get shoes.

"Fancia, you're not listening." It was true. I didn't want to hear what he was saying. He was telling me about Zhenia.

Her SS man's superior officer had threatened him with a court-martial for "fraternizing" with a "subhuman" Jew. The SS man had vindicated himself by driving her to the town square, where he threw her out of the truck "like a sack of potatoes," shouting, "Run, dirty whore!" She tried to but did not get far. "He shot her in the back."

"You saw this?"

"Yes." The whole town was there, laughing and jeering. Jan's face, unshaven, gray—the eyes sunk deeper in their sockets than I had remembered—set into an expression devoid of pity or anything else. "They tore her clothes off and . . ." His voice gave out.

He held both my hands in his, and as I looked down at the dirt encrusted on my skin and under my fingernails, I thought of Zhenia's hands the day of her sixteenth birthday. Her parents had given her a gold ring with a tiny ruby which she put on her middle finger, since it was too big for any of the others.

Jan took a salmon-colored scarf printed with a geometric design out of his pocket. "It's Zhenia's," he said. Stasiek, he explained, had put it aside for me when her things were given away to Ukrainian militiamen and peasants. It was not a scarf I recognized—something German, good nubby silk. I held it to my nose to inhale the faint scent of perfume, drawn from a subtle mix of flowers, which clung to it—the last evidence I would ever have of Zhenia's life.

Jan, who had always dragged me up from the depths of despair, sat there looking so forlorn that I felt I had to do something. "Let's lie down," I said.

He stood up. "I'm going out with a girl, the daughter of my father's friend." He spoke as if repeating a lesson he'd learned, though not very well.

"What do you want me to say? Congratulations?"

"Look, you know I don't want to. It's you I love. I'm still known as a 'Jewish uncle.' At my cousin's funeral, the priest came right out and said I wasn't needed there. Nobody has enough to eat. This girl's family is well-off." He spelled it out for me as I sat there, the tears running down my cheeks. I didn't want to use Zhenia's scrap of silk to wipe them off, so I let them run.

"You're not coming anymore?"

He kissed me. He belonged to someone else now. It had occurred to me once or twice before that he might have another girlfriend.

At the barn door, even after he opened it a crack, he came back and took me in his arms. He kissed me again. So, he'd lost all hope.

"What's the news?" my father asked as I crawled back into our coop.

"Not much." I told him that the Russian advance had halted. It hardly seemed to matter.

My father wanted to know how soon Jan would come again and I shook my head, but of course it was too dark to see. "What day?" He prodded me, his finger jabbing my shoulder like a stick. "What day?"

Now that Jan would not be coming anymore and whatever he might send would amount to next to nothing, even the effort of asking for war bulletins became absurd. No more pleading with Sidor to prevent Marynka from getting her pair of boots; no more saving a bit of bread for later. From that time on, we existed moment to moment.

Our clock, the chickens, informed us of the full turn of a day more or less, but sometimes I heard them and believed it was in a dream. Most of the time, if quizzed, I would not have been able to give the date or where I was. Back when I had been in hiding in Jan's attic, despite the reminders of a rooster and the comings and goings of a busy courtyard, I had often lost parts of mornings or afternoons; now I could not keep hold of days except in hourless batches. It seems to me that I must have stopped thinking and was existing on a battery that required the most minimal charge.

I knew my name and that my parents and Arthur were within arm's reach. They seemed less palpable than my vivid imaginings of that earlier time when I had lived at home and went to school. I'd see myself, perpetually thirteen, wandering around the garden and cleverly evading my mother's commands to come and help her in the house. It seemed vitally important that I remain alone and not reveal my hiding place in the lumber pile. I'd fear my book was lost, but then it always turned up and I would be floating in the world of a story that never came to an end.

I tried desperately to keep my eyes open in the murk of the hiding place, since keeping them closed, an easier choice, led to restless sleep. Waking from either a catnap or a longer sleep left me in a shattered state. I frequently woke with the same inner vista: a bare tree standing alone in the tundra after a cataclysmic storm, one twisted branch on the icy ground still tossing in the wind.

Each time I floated into full consciousness after sleep or lolled out from limbo, I registered faint surprise that my body was not yet a corpse, that my life wasn't over yet. My mother still passed a "wash rag" to me once in a while on which she dribbled a few drops of water so I could wipe my face, but I refused it.

Since my rational mind had absconded, and only the vestigial tic, the after-twitch of what had governed me, remained, I have no recollection of that time, and I can only present it as analogous to the apathy that takes over when a person with incontrovertible evidence of impending death, and assurance that nothing can be done to reverse it, lies back on the pillow and sails on.

VI

Liberation

(March 1944–July 1945)

Chapter Fifty-eight

ONE DAY SIDOR BROUGHT us a bowl of water in which beets had been boiled, saying it was all he could give us. I heard in his choked voice how much this pained him. "Such a comfortable house you had," he said, "and now you're squirming in that rat-hole."

Then his own chord of despair frightened him. "Don't do anything rash." Suicide was on his mind. Some Jews had bought cyanide pills with their last *zloty*, and he didn't know if we had any. Sidor figured that Ulanowski had supplied us with pills through Jan.

I had brought up the cyanide alternative before my parents left for the ghetto, but my father had been adamantly against it. When my father and I had talked about it, I still had the conviction, which seemed naive now, that making one's death an act of will had a noble ring to it. Though it would have saved us a year of torment, by enduring in our way we at least had not hurt Jan and Sidor. For all of us, religion forbade it. Now the act had lost any note of defiance or courage. Suicide had become rhetoric long before Sidor brought us the beet water. Now it was no longer necessary. Same result, just takes a little longer.

Sidor told us that a neighbor had asked for advice. When some

Jews had asked him to hide them, the man had consulted a Gypsy fortune-teller, who had encouraged him to do it. Now the fortune-teller had been killed. Should he drive the Jews out? My father inquired how Sidor had responded. "Keep them," he had told the neighbor. "With the fortune-teller dead, you no longer have to worry that she will denounce you and them." And the neighbor went home happy, Sidor said.

One day early in March, Marynka came at noon, and the light gushing in through the opening, though filtered by the window-less barn, hurt my eyes. She asked us to come out and eat a bowl of potato soup which was still steaming on the trough. My mother said not to go, but my father pushed Arthur and me out, and she followed us.

"Burial," said Marynka, "costs money—the wagon, the horse, the coffins. If you turn yourselves in, I'll see that you have a decent funeral."

I stared at her. I couldn't laugh or cry. My father said nothing. Finally my mother put down her spoon. "You know we have nothing. Why are you torturing us?"

Marynka said that we had things stashed away, probably with Jan or Ulanowski. "I bet you have jewels buried in the cellar."

My mother assured her that she had gotten the last of our jewelry.

Thinking of all the times I had imagined that in a few minutes I would be shot, my body defiled and then thrown into a mass grave, I found the idea of a funeral more like a ludicrous joke than an attempt at extortion.

"Marynka," my father said, handing her the empty soup bowl, "we're going back in now, and I promise not to mention this to Sidor." He knew she was afraid of Sidor; he had beaten her many times, and once he had almost beaten her to death.

"We'll see who has the last laugh," she muttered as she sealed us back in.

That night the temperature fell, and the quiet in the chicken yard told us it was snowing.

Three days passed before Sidor brought another bowl of soup. It had been more than two months now since the Russians had taken the city of Sarni and fought their way to the Dniester River. In a few days, perhaps even a few hours, Sidor said, the Russians would arrive.

Marynka came by with a bowl of sour milk. I ate it and fell asleep immediately.

A heavy rumble and shouting voices woke me. "Tanks," my father said. We didn't know whether they were German ones in retreat or Russian ones on the offensive. It seemed like a long time until Sidor came and removed the cover of the coop, but he didn't motion us to come out. Yes, it was the Red Army, but there were groups of Germans on the run who'd be happy to use their last bullets on Jews.

Some firm raps on the barn door stopped Sidor in mid-word. He closed the coop opening, and I could hear him tossing a few bales of hay against it. We heard the barn door open. German voices came nearer and mingled with Sidor's. Obviously they had shoved past him. Cut off from their unit, they asked to stay in the barn until nightfall. Sidor told them it was impossible, the Russians had already requisitioned it. "See, we have no guns," one said. Sidor stood his ground. "At least give us some bread," another said.

We heard the barn door close as Sidor led them to the house. Germans begging for bread sparked our spirits more than the vision of a thousand tanks passing by our door.

Chapter Fifty-nine

I BURNED TO LEAVE the hiding place. Something in me shouted to Sidor to let me out. It was an eternity until he came by. I crawled out, a worm, a spineless thing, and lay on the straw while Sidor hopped up and down with delight.

"You should have seen them," he said of the retreating German soldiers. "Dogs with their tails between their legs. Dirty, one of them wounded, bleary-eyed. I directed them to the forest." And he laughed so hard that I would have liked to join him but I couldn't. "The *Banderowtzi*"—the roaming "partisan" gangs that had arrived in the region from the forest—"will take care of them," he said.

Sidor went to Ulanowski to find out what was going on, and whether the war was, indeed, over. He brought home some butter Jan had given Ulanowski for us. Sitting at the kitchen table eating the gruel Marynka had enriched with Jan's butter, I looked at the room and the faces I knew so well and felt neither glad or sad. The phrase "it's over" was as empty as the prayer of gratitude to God my mother instructed us to say with her. Marynka and Sidor knelt down in front of the picture of Jesus to give thanks.

"I don't believe it," I said. "Maybe they'll come back." The only response I could muster to the news that the war was over was skepticism, which everyone jeered at except my father. Still, he decided that we could sleep in the attic, not in the hiding place. Foul hole that it was, Sidor thought to seal it up in case more fugitives came poking around and found it. But why bother, I thought. No animal except rats, who were old tenants, would enter that hellhole.

"The only way to clean it is with fire," I told him.

"Burn it," Arthur said. They were the first words he'd spoken for I don't know how long.

"It saved our lives," my father said.

I looked at Sidor, Marynka, and Hania. They and Jan. And Stasiek. And Ulanowski. All of them had saved us. What about them? Did only God and the hiding place get the credit?

Just before dawn, Aunt Sophia, Uncle Zygmunt, and Dolek arrived from a neighboring village. Their hiding place had been less than 3 kilometers away, but it had taken their weak legs several hours to walk that far. We looked at each other, pitying the emaciated creatures we saw before us. The skin around their eyes looked as if it had been bruised by a fist. Do I have those eyes, I wondered. What difference did it make? Looking at anything or anyone was an effort, an unreasonable demand, and so I fixed my gaze on the ground.

Uncle Zygmunt, Aunt Sophia, and Dolek slept on the dirt floor near the stove, which was seldom lit since wood was scarce. Marynka stumbled over them in the morning dimness—on purpose, Aunt Sophia said—which I doubted, since they were lying in the bit of space that Marynka had to cross when she got out of bed.

"She delights in our misery," Aunt Sophia whispered, and recounted the "spiteful" way Wasil had treated them. "Once a month he brought a pail of water so I could wash our clothes." Once a month! Ours hadn't been washed in six months! Aunt Sophia's contempt for "peasants" helped keep her mind off the lack of food, bed, and blankets.

Marynka's flour substitute, made of roots, resembled the powder used for concrete. She absently dragged her fingers back and forth through it as if it were water and then tipped the canister for us to see the white worms that stuck to the bottom of the sieve. Turning it upside down, she gave it a few whacks to shake the last of the flour out and made a batter, which she boiled because there was no fat to fry it in. Each of us got a dumpling. There was nothing to scavenge for in the thawing fields, not even rotted potatoes. All the chickens had been bartered or eaten.

A few days later, while sitting in the kitchen and sewing my father's jacket—which was already patched in dozens of places—I tuned in and out of the men's discussion. Uncle Zygmunt said they had to risk going to Skala to find food and a place to stay. Sidor cautioned against it, but my father, reluctant at first, agreed to go when it got dark.

"I'll go," I said. I knew all the shortcuts across streams and over fields and the back alleys which cut out of the main roads. Adept at procuring food before we had gone into hiding, I also had the advantage of being able to speak Russian, German, Ukrainian, or Polish in case I was stopped. True, I didn't have any ID papers, but I could say the partisans had taken them. I went over to my father and, taking his hand, gave my promise: "I'll be back tomorrow night."

"Out of the question," he said. "Asking for it," Sidor added, meaning rape by the Russians. No woman was safe during the first wave of oncoming troops. I said I'd wear Sidor's pants and my father's jacket. "Cut my hair," I ordered Marynka. She looked at my father for a cue, but he shook his head.

"She stays here," he said to Sidor, and he made Sidor swear to guard us with his life. We were to remain in the attic, and Hania should stay with us there, he said.

I was convinced I would be just as vulnerable in the house as on the road. *Banderowtzi* swooped down on village or town and took what they wanted. No sport short of obliterating a German division would give them more pleasure than to roister through this place and kill Jews.

Suddenly I was no longer the tractable daughter. I decided to slip out at dawn when everyone was still asleep.

Chapter Sixty

I GROPED MY WAY down the stairs from the attic after a few hours of sleep. "Zygmunt and your father left an hour ago," Aunt Sophia informed me.

Later in the morning, the sky cracked into pieces, at least that's how it sounded. I ran out to Sidor in the courtyard. Above our heads, an aerial battle lit up the sky with swathes of fire and smoke as planes zigged and zagged toward and away from each other. Neither of us knew a German plane from a Russian one until Arthur pointed out which was which: this one had a swastika, the other a hammer-and-sickle; he could spot the insignia when the planes came in low.

My mother dragged Arthur back into the house, but Sidor and I stood there in the deafening roar, watching a plane catch fire here or another nose-dive there. It looked like there were more Russian planes, and they eventually chased the struggling Luftwaffe away.

I worried that the Germans were still not defeated. Perhaps they had come back to Skala. Sidor said my father had a good nose for trouble but this time he'd "jumped the gun." Annoyed with Sidor for voicing my dread, I said, "Look, there's no food in the house. He'll come back or send Jan."

Sidor picked up a stiff old harness and began to polish the buckles with his sleeve. The buckles were badly corroded. "Jan won't come around for a while," he said.

"Why not?"

"I didn't tell you. The last time he was here, after he left he ran into a German patrol, and they beat him to a pulp. He's not going to come again until he's sure the Germans are gone."

Jan was in considerable danger, but not only from the Germans. The Russians, said Sidor, considered the Ukrainian militiamen collaborators, and some had disappeared along with the Germans. Jan's militia buddies were waiting to turn on him, to beat him up for all the times he was nowhere to be found when they went out hunting for Jews. "And the *Banderowtzi* would love to get their hands on a 'Jewish uncle.' "

Sidor put a brotherly arm around me. "His mother and girlfriend watch him day and night." He threw the harness against the wall.

"How can he help my father if he's . . . ," and I had trouble finding one word to cover all my worries.

"If he can he will," Sidor said.

There was only one thing to do. "I'm going to Skala," I said.

"Not if I can help it." The determination in Sidor's eyes left no doubt that he meant it.

That night I told Aunt Sophia and Dolek to take my father's and my place in the attic. I wanted to be awake when my father and uncle returned. I sat at the kitchen table and got up to shake myself out of sleep whenever I began to doze off. At dawn Sidor came to sit beside me. "It's too soon," he said, urging me to get some rest.

Marynka gave me a sweater of Hania's to unravel, and I sat there watching the small wool torso on the table shrivel bottom upwards as the ball of wool grew in my hands. There wasn't enough to make her another sweater, but I decided to start one anyway to appease my restless fingers. Hania sat beside me, and I put her on my lap to guide her hands as she tried to knit a few stitches. For each one on the needle she dropped two. "Don't worry about it," I reassured her.

The day dragged on until Marynka put some onions on the

table. "Here's salt," she said. "Drink lots of water." It worked. My stomach stopped badgering me and I began to knit again.

Arthur and Dolek found a rusty old bicycle wheel in the yard which they brought in and took turns spinning for its creaky gyrations. Hania sat down beside them, hoping for a turn, but neither boy offered to give her one. "Take a turn," I called to her, and she looked from one boy to the other to gauge whether she could risk it.

Those three days when no word came from my father and Uncle Zygmunt were like the time in the hiding place after the typhus crisis, when my inert body in its crouch and cramp seemed weightless, freed to fly back and forth just below the ceiling of an unknown room. I seemed to be in that room again, but at times I crashed against the wall and fell to the muddy floor. My mind raced continuously, making scenarios of my father's activities while my body, thin as it was, felt heavy, a burden to keep stoked, a thing which by virtue of gender made me a target of the Russians and thus kept me as stultified as a slug.

Chapter Sixty-one

LATE IN THE AFTERNOON of the third day, I set out for Skala. If I wanted to use the byways I had learned from Jan, I had to go while some light remained for me to see the landmarks. Once I got out of sight of Sidor's house, some untapped strength helped me to jump over a stile and a high, jagged fence. At one point I had to stop in a ditch and retie the rags on my feet. Had I asked Sidor or Marynka for their shoes, they would have guessed my purpose.

I saw a peasant with a sack on his shoulders walking along a parallel path a few yards away. I knew he couldn't see me if I flattened myself in the ditch. But the instant after I stepped into it I jumped up again and ran toward him. The country jacket and sack had almost fooled me. His loping gait identified Uncle Zygmunt. His bony, unshaven face, seasoned by hard work, could have been a peasant's, but his long incarceration had given him a bleached look.

I led him to the ditch. "Where's Papa?" His fingers, as he tapped my hand to gesture "wait, wait, wait," had a bloodless touch.

"Fancia, take me to Sidor's," he said in such a feeble tone that I could not refuse.

Before I hoisted the sack on my shoulders, I peeked in. It was filled with straw. I left it lying there, neck gaping, a ready bed for field mice.

We sat at Sidor's kitchen table as my uncle told his story. He and my father had entered Skala three days before and had gone to the marketplace. Jan had run up to my father, happy to see him again. In the marketplace square, my father and Uncle Zygmunt had found other Jews who had emerged from hiding, and they shared information on who had survived and who had been killed.

My father and uncle went over to a group of Russian soldiers who were splashing their faces at a fountain, Uncle Zygmunt reported. "Your father rushed up to them, fell on his knees, kissed their boots, and began embracing them and thanking them for liberating us. 'We're Jews,' he said. They didn't seem to care, but they gave us two loaves of bread." Uncle Zygmunt pulled a quarter of a loaf from his pocket and set it on the table.

Then, in front of the Russians and everyone else, my father had vowed revenge—not only for Leo and Misia but for all the Jews who had been murdered, said Uncle Zygmunt. I had never heard my father speak vengefully, but it was possible that making a vow of revenge was the only way he felt he could go on after hearing about Leo and Misia's murder.

"I could see some women watching all this from behind their curtains, and some men stopping and pointing at Benjamin and me. 'Zhyds,' they said. One called out, 'As cheeky as ever.' And another yelled, 'I thought we'd gotten them all.' "

My father, Uncle Zygmunt continued, hung around the Russians, listening to what they had to say about the Red Army's activities.

"I tried to tear Benjamin away," Uncle Zygmunt said, looking at my mother, "but I couldn't budge him. I told him I would meet him at the fountain around midnight, and left.

"That was the last time I saw him, three nights ago—in front of the fountain talking to a group of Russian soldiers."

I asked Zygmunt if he'd returned to the fountain at midnight, as arranged.

"It must have been around then. There were no bells, so I had to guess the time. I waited for hours, two or three at least, and finally went to Jan. Jan—what a beating that man's been given!—took me to his barn and told me that Benjamin had been there earlier and left."

"Where to?" I asked.

"To Ulanowski. I stayed in the barn all that day. Jan said it was foolish to walk around in daylight." The Germans, encircled by the Russians who had arrived in Skala, had broken through the lines, killing Jews in town right and left. "Ulanowski had warned that two Jews he knew, Finio Finkel and Chaim Gottes-feld"—not a relative, but a member of a Skala family who lived on the road to the brewery and whom we always referred to as "the other Gottesfelds"—"had been killed in the last few days."

"So, is that where he is, at Ulanowski's?" my mother asked.

"I don't know where he is."

Sidor shook his head. "Did you go to Ulanowski?"

My uncle nodded. "Yes. Ulanowski said Benjamin never came to his house."

"So where *is* he?" my mother asked.

We stared at Uncle Zygmunt as he shrugged his shoulders. Then he shrugged again. "I stayed in Jan's barn the second day, too. That night, as I wandered about, I met a neighbor of Jan's who said yes, he'd seen Benjamin leave Jan's place that night, but that's all he knew. I went back to Ulanowski. Ulanowski said maybe he went to Father Derewienko. I don't know. I didn't go to him. And then Fancia found me on the way back." He patted my hand with his cold one. If there was blood coursing in its veins, it must have been like slush in an icy stream.

Chapter Sixty-two

SIDOR RETURNED FROM THE MARKET in Skala the next day with a small sack of cornmeal obtained on credit, to be paid for with hay in the summer. We needed food, yes, but I had sent him to Skala to find out where my father was.

The moment I saw the grim look on his face, I had a terrible feeling of foreboding that my father was dead.

Sidor reported that he had gone to see Jan and Ulanowski and had corroborated Uncle Zygmunt's story: my father had been to see Jan, left to go to Ulanowski, never arrived there, and after that, no trace of him remained.

"What does Ulanowski say?" I asked Sidor.

"Ulanowski is very upset. About your father, yes, but also about Dora." Ulanowski had hidden Dora, a smart and very sweet and affectionate girl I knew who had been in Shimek's class in school. Her parents and sister had been deported during the *aktsia*. At some point, she had found shelter with Ulanowski.

"Some women threw stones at her when she stepped out on the street, and one of them hit her in the eye." Ulanowski blamed himself for not stopping Dora from leaving his house.

Sidor added that another young girl had "slipped out of hiding yesterday," and he hesitated before continuing, "well, she's dead." How naive of me to think that the move from the coop to the kitchen meant anything had changed! Almost all the Ukrainians and Poles wanted the Jews dead whether the Germans were gone or not.

Ulanowski had talked of the "false Liberation." The Russians, Sidor said, were only an advance force. "The Germans are back in Skala." They had returned on the second day of my father's absence. "There's fighting going on right now north of town," he reported. The Jews were in a panic and ran to seek hiding wherever they could. Some had joined the Russians as they retreated from town.

A spasm of hope gripped me: perhaps my father had gone with the Russians, maybe he had been forced to go with them as a local engineer. Perhaps he was caught somewhere in a battle. Maybe wounded. Wounded is better than dead. Finio Finkel's and Chaim Gottesfeld's bodies had been found on the street, but not my father's. Maybe he was still alive!

Sidor took my hand. "It's not over yet," he said. He told us that Jan would come by tomorrow and perhaps he would have some news.

When Uncle Zygmunt heard this, he, Aunt Sophia, and Dolek went into the old hiding place in the chicken coop and asked Sidor not to tell Jan they were hiding there.

Jan arrived the next morning. He had a bandage over his ear, and when he spoke I saw that one of his teeth had been knocked out. The small bouquet of early purple and white flowers he held out to me looked almost wilted, but they perked up in a beaker of water.

He said that the battle was over, and the Russians were now entrenched in Skala.

"Where's my father?" I spoke with such challenge that he answered me sharply. He didn't know. He had made inquiries and no one knew.

"When he got to my house," Jan said, "he was crying. He had just heard about Leo and Misia. He told me he was going to get the guy who killed them. Maybe someone else heard him say that."

"Speculations!" I said. I looked Jan in the eye: "You shouldn't have let him leave your place."

Jan sprang up. "Let him leave? I couldn't stop him! He said he had to find food. I told him I would get some in the morning, but he said no, that he was going to Father Derewienko while it was still dark."

That made no sense. Why would my father go to see the priest, an arch-collaborationist, when the Germans were back in town and fighting was raging? It didn't sound like something my father—whose strong instinct for survival had saved us on several occasions—would do.

Jan's story also contradicted what Uncle Zygmunt had said Jan told him originally: that my father had gone to Ulanowski.

But Uncle Zygmunt wasn't there to confront Jan; he and his family were still hiding in the chicken coop.

Jan tried to comfort me, but I pulled away from him. I was going to Father Derewienko immediately, I announced.

I waited alone in the priest's parlor—Jan would not enter the church he had been kicked out of—until he finished his duties. He looked genial and healthy. His cheeks were red, and the war's privation had not diminished his big belly. He sat with folded hands as I told him that he must tell me what had happened to my father no matter how bad the news was.

"My child," said Father Derewienko, "your father never arrived here." There had been a battle north of town, and he suggested that I go look at the bodies that still lay unburied in the fields. I did not mention the ring my father had given him for safekeeping three years before, and neither did he.

Jan offered to go with me to the field of battle to see if I could find my father's body. As we approached the area, the stench of rotting bodies lodged in my nose and throat before the hundreds of dead came into view. Jan tore his handkerchief in half, and we tied the pieces over our mouths and noses.

In one corner, an unfilled crude mass grave next to German battle debris indicated that the Germans had hurried away, leaving their soldiers' bodies to rot. Many were very young, Hitler's last fighters. There were also bodies of Russian soldiers and of civilians. Many of the bodies had the boots removed from their feet. Numerous hands had the ring finger cut off. Randomly scattered, the bodies were hard to sidestep. We looked at each face together as we turned the body over, but after a few dozen we split up.

Some incalculable strength held me up, pushed me on, and kept me calm even at the moment when I saw the button I was sure I had sewn on my father's jacket near a figure that lay face down.

I screamed and Jan rushed over. There was no shirt under the jacket, just a torso that overfilled it, making the buttons pop off. Perhaps he was a German deserter who had thrown his uniform away. Jan thought he was one of the *Banderowtzi* who had come from the forest to loot in town. I bent down to pick up the button. The thread trailing from it was brown. I had used black thread. Jan took the button out of my hand and threw it away. "It's a common button. A mistake. Come. We'll keep on looking."

None of the other corpses or body parts gave a hint of my father. He had vanished.

All I wanted to do was get washed. If it had been warmer, I would have gone to the river. Jan wanted me to come to the hiding place in his barn after dark to bathe. I refused. His mother and sister had not changed. No, I told him, I would go back to Sidor's, and he needn't come with me. He insisted that a woman wasn't safe walking alone when so many Russians were around.

"Why weren't you so persuasive with my father?" I asked. I was furious with him. "You killed him! You let him walk out of your barn door."

"Is that what you think?"

We walked back to Sidor's using the back routes. Neither of us said a word. The dead bodies on the battlefield kept juxtaposing themselves in my mind with wishful thoughts of Jan wrestling with my father to keep him in the barn. After all he'd done for us, why couldn't he have done this one last thing?

At Sidor's door he turned to walk back. He did not say goodbye.

Chapter Sixty-three

TWO DAYS LATER, the six of us left Sidor's and split up to investigate whichever Gottesfeld and Wasserman houses had not been occupied by Ukrainians, looking for one with a roof, floors, and a door.

My mother and I found some Ukrainians living in our home. In my Wasserman grandparents' house, the windows were gone.

Aunt Sophia had gone right to her childhood home. Although the windows of Grandfather Azriel's house had no glass, they had boards nailed over them. We joined her there and settled in. Two sisters we had known casually before the war had appropriated one room. My uncle, aunt, and Dolek took another that miraculously still had a double bed in it. My mother, Arthur, and I improvised sleeping arrangements in the only other habitable room, the kitchen. My mother put together the remains of some old beds for her and Arthur. I slept on blankets on the floor.

"So, where is he now, when we need him—your bridegroom?" my aunt asked. Her eyes signaled merriment, but her voice trailed off into scorn. I had no intention of discussing Jan with her, and asked what we needed him for. "To help make a hiding place," my uncle said. Even if the Germans had not come back, there were Ukrainians and Poles ready to finish Hitler's job.

"I'll tell you why he's not here," my aunt said, addressing my mother. "He killed Benjamin and he can't face us."

"No," said my mother. "Benjamin's in Russia. He's alive. I heard at the market that some Jews went off with the advance party of Russians when they retreated." She looked at Arthur as if to answer him. "Papa will write us. Or he'll send a message."

My mother put on the table the small cache of beans she had managed to wheedle from a farmer. I was carefully sieving through them for stones when the sisters, who had swollen bellies just like ours, came in—they too had some beans in a small bag. Now the question was, who would use the single cooking pot first? "Cook them all together," I suggested. The women looked at me as if I had spoken curse words. We had six stomachs to appease, and the sisters only had two.

The older one, in a gesture of conciliation, told me that the Russians were looking for a girl to work in the office of the Soviet military command, located in the building of the former Polish garrison.

I got the job because I knew Russian and other Slavic languages and also because I was not a Pole or a Ukrainian. My co-workers were all Ukrainian girls who were eventually phased out.

What we had to do was make lists of men of military age the Russians could draft into the Red Army—the war was still going on—and write letters. There were no typewriters, and good handwriting was important.

I also had to write autobiographies for the officers. They were constantly required to update their autobiographies, but many— even the top commanders—were illiterate. Some had acquired merit as a result of actions during the civil war. Others had been promoted as heroes for having distinguished themselves in recent battles with the Germans.

While working in the office, I met my Communist cousin, who had returned to Skala and found out that his family had been murdered. He advised me to go to Russia and study medicine there.

My first morning on the job, a message came in that Jan was in jail. All the Ukrainian militiamen had been arrested as collaborators.

Chapter Sixty-four

IT UPSET ME TO SEE Jan lying on a pallet of straw too small for him in a filthy cell the size of a small cubicle. I'd never seen him hurt anyone, and even Uncle Zygmunt, who had disapproved of my father's trust in Jan, admitted that Jan had never been seen harming a Jew. "Looting, maybe."

I put my hand through the grates of the cell and gave Jan some white bread I had obtained at lunch in trade for the coarse black bread we got at the bakery. I had put a little honey on top of the bread, and my fingers were sticky from it.

I went to see Jan in jail once a day. I didn't tell anyone at home that I had been to see him. My mother asked me where he was, but I said I didn't know. One time when I visited him, he looked as if he'd been beaten.

In a way, I was glad he was in jail. Reprisals against Poles and Ukrainians who had aided Jews were being reported through the grapevine. Jan himself told me about a Polish friend of my father's, a man I knew, who had given sanctuary to Jews in Czortkow. He had been stopped while driving in his car on the outskirts of town. The car was set on fire with kerosene while he was inside, and he was burned so badly that he died.

Once when I went to see Jan, his sister was visiting him.

Before I turned to leave I heard her say to him, "She isn't worth it, your little Jewess."

She made very sure that I heard what she said.

I had seen his sister once before this when I went to her house to ask her to give back the suitcase of silk dresses and suits my mother had left with her. Of course, she had denied knowing anything about it. Later, I found out that she and Jan's mother had made numerous visits to the headquarters of the Ukrainian militia during the war urging them to find our family. His mother wanted me dead.

On the way home from one of my jailhouse visits with Jan, some former classmates from Polish elementary school stopped me. "What, you're back?" they exclaimed, as if some dirt and debris swept into the sewer had miraculously reappeared on the sidewalk.

So far, fifty out of the fifteen hundred Jews who had lived in Skala before the German invasion had come back. For most of the townspeople it was too many.

Marysia came to see us in Grandfather Azriel's house. She kissed Arthur, just as she had when she came to the attic of Jan's barn after the *aktsia*. "Get the hell out of here," I told her. "You didn't want to know from us before, you didn't even bring us one rotten potato. We don't need you." I threw her out of the house.

We learned that Suza and Munio had been murdered a few weeks before the Liberation. They had been hiding in a little village. Munio was working there as a dentist, making teeth for the Gestapo men and for the Ukrainians.

The SS men took a liking to him. When they got wind that there were orders to kill him and Suza, they warned him, "You'd better go, we'll be coming back in an hour." When the Germans returned, the couple were still in their house. They had not had enough time to find someone to hide them, or perhaps they had tried but had been turned down. With the war drawing to an end, maybe they thought that the Gestapo wouldn't go out of their way to kill two more Jews. But they did.

My mother and I went to the village and asked the Ukrainians what had happened to Suza and Munio, and were told they had been shot and thrown into a ditch. They refused to tell us where the ditch was. We went from ditch to ditch, looking for traces of their bodies, but never found them.

After a week in jail, Jan was released and began to accompany me home from the Soviet headquarters as he had done when I worked for the manager of the count's estate. Once in a while the Ukrainian girls in the office whispered just loud enough for me to hear as we passed, "What does he see in her?" "He risked his life for her?"

Jan ignored the remarks. He'd take my arm or my hand to show how he felt about me. I knew he was getting lots of flak at home. He told me that his mother and sister had suggested he move to another town because no one in Skala would want him to repair their shoes.

I'll never forget the eyes of the Ukrainian girls seated at desks at the Russian headquarters the time I submitted a deposition for Jan to keep him out of the army. As I entered the commander's anteroom, half a dozen girls stared at me so hard that I froze in my tracks. "You came back," one said as if spitting at me. "Look at her," another one said, "she has the nerve to show her face." Had their eyes been brooms I would have been swept out in a moment.

I walked right past them into the commander's office. He was not impressed that Jan had saved the lives of four Jews, but permitted me to fill out a form.

"Why are you so interested in this man?" He had a sophisticated, almost debonair manner.

"I'm his girlfriend."

"He's too good to fight for Russia?" he asked, elevating an eyebrow. Jan, I told him, had risked his life for years to keep us out of the clutches of the Germans and deserved some respite. I knew that the gift of a watch would expedite the transaction, but I had none. I told the commander I could guarantee a vial of mercury for him the next time a pharmacist friend of mine received a delivery. Mercury—a cure for VD—was even more prized than wristwatches.

Moizesevich had beckoned me into his pharmacy the first week we came out of hiding. He was so happy to see me alive. He had on several occasions during the war supplied my father with medicine through Jan, and Aunt Sophia through Wasil. He was troubled that my father had disappeared.

Moizesevich had not had an easy time during the war. An Armenian who by name and looks could well have been a Jew, he had repeatedly been forced to prove otherwise by lowering his pants.

"All the Russians have gonorrhea," he told me that day. "Syphilis the Russians have too." He warned me not to let any of them touch me.

Either my promise to the commander worked or my allusion to a cure for VD hurt his dignity. Abruptly, he signed a sheet of paper, indicating that I was to take it, and turned his back to open a file. When I walked out through the anteroom under the eyes of the Ukrainian girls, I felt cloaked in a cape of triumph. I tried to slam the door behind me, but it was too heavy, and all I heard was the creak of rusty hinges over a babble of voices.

The fear of conscription into the Russian army stirred anxiety at home, too. It was the topic of conversation one day when Sidor dropped in, as he did once in a while, always with some item, usually food. This time he came to say that he had obtained an exemption because he had a job in the vodka distillery, which the Russians had geared up into full production.

Sidor declined my offer to make a deposition in his favor in case it should prove to be necessary. "They like me, the Russians," he said. It became clear from the conversation that he had managed to purloin a stock of vodka to sell privately. "You're not smart enough to cheat the Russians," I told him. He laughed: "Marynka says the same thing."

Chapter Sixty-five

WHEN THE JEWS who had "run away with the Russians" during the "false Liberation" returned and told my mother that my father had not been with them, she came up with a new theory: Yes, her husband was dead, and only one man could have killed him—Dzsisiak, Jan's ex-fiancée's father. Early in the German occupation, when Jan broke his engagement with Dzsisiak's daughter, her father had let it be known that he would avenge the insult. My mother decided that he had. "Everyone knows he's a drunk," she added.

The next Sunday afternoon, as we walked to Dzsisiak's house—which was not far from Jan's and, like his, near the old Jewish cemetery—my mother cued me: "You must make him see that we only want to hear the truth and that we won't report him." She had designated me spokesperson, but once we were sitting on the stiff horsehair sofa in his second-best parlor, she took over.

Even though Dzsisiak was a wealthy landowner and she an impoverished widow, she addressed him in the familiar second-person singular: "My husband was seen coming into your house and never heard from since." Dzsisiak, a burly man with a pipe clenched in his mouth, said it was a lie, Benjamin Gottesfeld had not crossed his threshold. She wouldn't prosecute, my mother told him, she just wanted him to admit his crime and she would forgive him.

"You Jews are worse than ever," he said.

My eyes traveled across shelves crowded with porcelain figurines and vases and rested on a gray earthen vessel inscribed with a large blue six-pointed star.

"My daughter didn't need Jan," he said. "She's well-fixed and has a bouncing baby boy." He looked me over, appraising my thin body for motherhood, and stood up. "Too many of you have come back," he said.

The second outing my mother decided we must make was to Father Derewienko. We didn't go to his church, as I'd done with Jan, but to his beautiful house next-door to it.

Without much formality, my mother demanded that he return the diamond ring my father had deposited with him. "My dear lady," he said, a grin on his shiny red face, "the ring is not here. Your husband came to get it himself." He threw the doors of his large cabinet open as if inviting her to search through it.

"When?"

"The first week in March," he said.

That was impossible, my mother told him, because we had been in hiding at Sidor's at the time and he couldn't have gone to Skala.

The priest's expression made it clear that he took offense at being called a liar. "Wait here," he said. He came back with a five-pound bag of white flour and told her it was to show that he forgave her for the accusation.

Uncle Zygmunt criticized my mother upon our return home for having "run off half-cocked" to engage in impulsive confrontations with Dzsisiak and Derewienko. She was "asking for trouble," he said.

His remarks were a sign of the conflict that had begun among the four of us. In our home, my father had always been head of the family. Now each of us—Zygmunt, Sophia, my mother, and I—considered ourselves in charge of its welfare.

The day we had walked from Sidor's to Skala, my uncle had

put his arm around my mother and said, "Now I have two wives and three children."

My mother suspected that my uncle still had some hides in safekeeping. "He could roll up a nice skin and go to Russian headquarters and get them to find out what happened to your father." I understood what she meant; the Russians had methods of extracting information from people.

"Find out from whom?" I asked.

"Jan," she said. Jan! How could my mother suggest that Jan be subjected to torture after he had saved our lives thousands of times!

"Papa was last seen alive in his house," she said.

Chapter Sixty-six

EXCEPT AT THE DEAD OF NIGHT, the kitchen was a hubbub of movement and chatter. My thoughts flew back to the coop at Sidor's, how we had sat scrunched together: a four-limbed hydra-monster quiescent for six months, how we could barely be roused, and then only if Rex barked fiercely.

Now the storm was over and yet the wind blew harder than ever. I lived in a flux of daily needs and no prospects. Sleeping on the kitchen floor, hungry, in rags, lice-ridden, a turtle with carapace torn from its back, I felt exposed, half-blinded, deadened by sun and air, ignored by the world.

My father's disappearance and probable death galvanized my mother—who had been helpless throughout the war—into improvising ways to keep us clothed and fed. She directed me to pry wood moldings from the doors and windows of the rooms to use for bartering in the market. Some wood I saved for cooking, but it was never enough to keep the house or even the kitchen warm.

The clamor in the market jarred my nerves; the pushing and screaming reminded me of the time I had gone for cucumbers and was nearly trampled by the starving mob—the time Jan had first appeared in my life.

One day Aunt Sophia heard of a shipment of coal for sale and we rushed to get some. After haggling over the price and paying with a stack of dismantled window frames, she heaved the sack on my back. My knees buckled and the sack fell off. Several more times she flung it on my back and I assured her that I could carry it, but after the fourth try I had to admit I couldn't do it. We divided it up, and I used my skirt as an auxiliary sack. A trickle of black perspiration ran down my chest, evidence of my feeble body's shame.

I knew I looked awful: I was extremely underweight, and my skin had the pimply lusterlessness it had acquired in the chicken coop. I still had lice, and Aunt Sophia continued to wash my hair with kerosene. And I had nothing decent to wear.

Aunt Sophia had found in the house a long, black shiny coat that had belonged to Grandfather Azriel and a black shawl of Grandmother Hinda's. I unraveled the shawl and knit sweaters for my mother, my aunt, and myself. Then Aunt Sophia got back two kimonos she had left in safekeeping with a non-Jew. Ske kept the blue kimono and gave me the black rayon one. I promised a seamstress a handknit sweater if she'd make it into a dress for me.

The day it was ready, Jan showed up with a pair of black grosgrain sandals. To me the white-accented stripes and platform soles spelled elegance. They showed off my pretty legs, Jan said. I loved the shoes and wore them everywhere except to bed. I refused to take them off even when I went with my aunt to sift through people's garbage for leavings to put in the soup.

One day, a woman ran after us in a back alley and pinched me to a halt. "Your shoes," she said. I was about to tell her that I hadn't stolen them when she continued, "I'd know those shoes anywhere. They were custom-made for my mother." Her mother had been killed. I had no idea how Jan had gotten the sandals—maybe he'd looted their home, maybe they had been given to him or to a friend to hide, maybe he'd bought them from a looter. I had never asked.

Aunt Sophia hurried me away from the alley.

Chapter Sixty-seven

SEPTEMBER, 1944. The new semester was about to begin in Czortkow, the nearest town with a functioning high school, and I wanted to finish my one remaining year of school and get my diploma.

Combing Czortkow to find a room for rent, my mother and I ran into her best friend, Mrs. Axelrod, who had attended business school with her. She was now a widow and lived with her bachelor brother. I do not know how or where they had survived. Since the brother, a doctor, had resumed his practice, and it gave them enough to live on, it was agreed that with the supplement of a handful of kasha now and then, I was welcome to live with them.

Although the Axelrods were nice to me, I didn't feel really comfortable living with them. The kasha my mother brought them from time to time hardly qualified as room-and-board, and I felt like a beggar in their house. And I was treated like a child. My mother had told Mrs. Axelrod that I was seventeen, not nineteen, and the widow considered it her duty to act as a surrogate mother to a minor. One of her maternal acts was to give me vigorous kerosene shampoos to try to get rid of the lice I still had months after the Liberation.

Still, Czortkow suited me. The mental stimulation of school-work in the morning exhilarated me after three years of not having a book to read nor pen and paper for writing. The system was basically the same as in the Russian high school in Borsz-czow—Marx, Lenin, military training, and encouragement to spy on fellow students: a few Jews and the rest Poles and Ukrainians.

My afternoon duties for the Russians in their military head-quarters, assigned by the school as "service," were similar to those I'd carried out in the Skala commander's office: writing letters and dictated autobiographies for dossiers the mostly illit-erate Russian officers had to constantly update. From time to time, an attractive officer would try to tempt me to visit a café with him, but I always turned him down.

Jan rented a room with a Ukrainian family in Czortkow soon after I arrived there. He told me the Russians were still arresting and rearresting militiamen, and that the harassment for his being a "Jewish uncle" had not abated. He had obviously found it very unpleasant to remain in Skala.

Jan always waited at the gate like a faithful dog to walk me home.

"Who's that man who comes to pick you up?" one of the girls asked me during lunch. "Are you related?"

"Oh, he's just a guy who helped my family."

"He's so old," another girl said.

Sometimes, after work, Jan and I would walk to the market-place, where the peasants had set up little booths with kerosene stoves on which they cooked *pirogen* which we would eat as we walked around. At other times, he'd come back home with me and sit in an armchair. Mrs. Axelrod would bring him a glass of tea while he watched me do my homework or listened to amusing tidbits I related to him from the day's dossiers. Sundays we always spent walking, stopping at a café for a treat before spending a few hours in his room.

We were still lovers, but I felt very conflicted about Jan—grateful to him for saving my life but tormented by the accusa-tion that he had killed my father. I had feelings for him but was more aware than ever of the great disparity in age, religion, and background. But I had no one to turn to for advice on what to do. My two best friends, Lotka and Zhenia, were dead. Shimek was dead. I felt isolated and alone.

Everybody in Czortkow knew about Jan and me, as they did in Skala; it was something of a scandal that he had saved me, that he was a "Jewish uncle," that he wasn't working—he was afraid to work for the Russians and kept a low profile—but spent a lot of time watching out for me, just like when we were under the boot of the Germans.

One sunny Sunday as Jan and I were walking across a deserted hill, he told me that his sister had written him a letter reporting what people in Skala were saying about a Polish fellow from Czortkow named Stephan. The case had caused an uproar in Czortkow, reverberating all the way back to Skala.

Stephan was already married when he fell in love during the war with a Jewish girl, a cosmetician who had studied in Vienna. Stephan had saved her and also her younger sister, a girl I'd gone to school with.

After the Liberation, Stephan wanted to leave his wife and live with his lover. (Being Catholic, he could not get a divorce.) But she fell in love with a Russian officer and married him.

Stephan went to her apartment and hanged himself there.

Jan said there was talk about prosecuting her.

I began to shiver. For a moment I thought I was back in the chilly dark of the hiding place. Jan sat down and motioned to me to come sit in the crook of his arm.

"I suppose your sister thinks the woman deserves to be killed."

"Taking her life will not bring Stephan back," he said. He chafed his hand up and down my arm to help keep me warm. "The Russian general is a powerful man. I don't think anything will happen to her."

I accepted Jan's jacket on my shoulders. "Why did your sister write you about this?"

Back in Skala, he said, people had started to make fun of him, saying it would soon be his turn to be abandoned by his Jewish lover. Neither of us spoke for a while. The stone I sat on was rapidly losing the heat of the afternoon's sun. I got up to go. Jan insisted I keep his jacket on.

"My sister," he said to me, "ended her letter with the words, 'When will *you* hang yourself?' "

Chapter Sixty-eight

I RETURNED TO SKALA when I received word that my mother had pneumonia. When I reached her bedside, I realized that agitation over my father's death, rather than disease, was making her ill.

"They say Jan did it."

"Who?"

"Everyone. People. Jan murdered your father."

I asked her if she believed it; she said yes, and that I should, too. "We're too naive," she said, adding that I didn't understand the depths of Ukrainian barbarity.

Were these the ravings of someone disoriented by fever or simply an effort to drive a wedge between Jan and me? She liked Jan, I knew that. But not for me. It astounded me that when Jan came to visit us, my mother treated him as one of the family, and yet when he was not in the room he was under suspicion of murder. He lived near the Jewish cemetery, she said; he could have axed the body into pieces and buried them in one of the plots. "The dogs wouldn't scratch there like in a yard," she said.

When I got back to Czortkow, I dreamt that my father's body had been buried somewhere and that I was compelled to find his grave. In the dream I searched cemeteries, scrambling over broken stones and ransacking graves, expecting Jan to come help me, but I always woke up before he arrived.

One day, when I came home late after being delayed at work, I found Jan in tears and Mrs. Axelrod patting his hands. Usually she greeted me with a smile, but this time she cast a somber look in my direction. I could see she was upset.

After Jan left, she told me that he'd blurted out his love for me and his fear that we would be parted. "He says you think he murdered your father. Is that true?"

I was angry with Jan for drawing Mrs. Axelrod into my private life. I told her it didn't matter what I thought. My father was dead. Jan had saved my family, and I was grateful.

The next day, after work, I told Jan I wanted to go to his room. Usually I sat on the bed, but today I chose the wooden chair. "You shouldn't have told Mrs. Axelrod about us."

I wanted him to look at me, but he concentrated on a spot on the wall.

"My aunt and uncle want me to come to live with them in Lvov." They had gone to Lvov around the time I went to Czortkow. Aunt Sophia, who spoke Polish, Russian, Ukrainian, German, and Hebrew, and had a sophisticated command of Yiddish, regretted that her schooling had been cut off early and was urging me to finish high school in Lvov. But her real motive, obviously, was to end my affair with Jan.

He looked up quickly. "Are you going?"

Another departure, another gamble. Saying good-bye to each other while in hiding and now daily at the door was as much a part of us as clasping hands. Missing him had become a habit, and yet often, while reading or walking alone, I felt exhilarated in a way that didn't occur when Jan and I were together.

The idea of going to live in a big city frightened me, and yet the chance to meet new people made it attractive. I thought of Lvov as a lake I could stick my toe into and watch the ripples fan out ahead of me. Yes, I might fall in and drown, I knew that, but on the other hand, I was also capable of learning to swim.

"The school is better in Lvov," I said. "And my mother wouldn't have to contribute to my upkeep."

I had expected him to advise me not to go. But suddenly he was all plans. His cousin Elena in Lvov had a spare room for him, and jobs were more readily available there. He promised to follow me in a month or so. I found his single-minded enthusiasm irritating, probably because I was trying to distance myself from him.

"You know," he said, "I care for you more than ever."

He got up and, with a gentle tug on my hand, tried to draw me toward the bed. "I have homework to do for tomorrow," I said.

He wrote down his cousin's address in Lvov in case I needed anything. As I watched him adjust his collar and jacket I noticed, as I had thousands of times, how the dexterity of his hands triumphed over the loss of two fingers. The touch of those hands had become as familiar as my own, and at that moment I longed for them to stroke me. We were standing in the same room but kissed as if we had already decided to part. We both cried.

The following Sunday I managed to arrange for a place in an army truck going to Lvov.

As I rode in the cab of the truck, I remembered the rides, years before, to and from the high school in Borszczow squashed under a lap robe between Russian soldiers and how their busy bear claws had worked to pry a space between my knees. Those ordeals with the Russians had angered me to curses and tears, but I hadn't known in my gut the fear of rape, as I did now.

The high-ranking Soviet officer who was the other passenger had offered me the window seat, but I declined. I decided that sitting in the middle, with the sober-faced driver to my left, might serve as a deterrent to the officer on my right, should he try anything. Of course, there was always the possibility that they were in cahoots and would take me to a deserted cul-de-sac. But the glum-faced officer made certain to leave several inches of space between us, and after a formal greeting, he ignored me.

Several hours later, coming out of a daze, I noticed that the truck was coming to a stop in a fairly large town. Empty barrels and litter in the square were evidence that a fair had been held there earlier in the day. Apologizing for the delay, the officer told me to get out of the truck and follow him. He took me to the back of an inn and instructed me to help an old woman who was filling up pails of water from a kettle.

I followed her to an inner room. Lit candles stood like sentinels around the nude body of a dead man lying on the table. "An officer," she said. "The third one in two weeks." Although the sight of the inert body upset me, it was the agonized face that disturbed me most. The man had died in great pain. He was probably no older than Jan.

"The *Banderowtzi*," she told me. "Like hawks," she said, flapping her arms to show how they flew in from the forest to catch their prey.

The woman directed me to do as she did, dipping a rag in the pail, then washing the corpse. We dressed him in a freshly laundered uniform, affixed his medals, and put rouge on his face. Then Russian soldiers put the body in an open casket and carried it the long way around the marketplace to the cemetery. A violinist following the entourage of soldiers played a funeral march by Chopin that would reverberate in my ears for years to come.

I stood between the driver and the officer, watching soldiers roll over a large stone to mark the grave. Two others had already been planted nearby. The townspeople stood close to their houses in silence.

Back in the truck after the burial, the officer took out a bottle of vodka and offered me a sip. I took it, hoping that food would be offered too. It wasn't. When we got to Lvov the officer instructed the driver to take me to my uncle and aunt's door. After I jumped down from the truck, the driver, whistling the Chopin melody, executed a screeching U-turn so that, as I stood there, I could receive the officer's correct, unsmiling salute.

Chapter Sixty-nine

I HAD WANTED TO BE in Lvov to test myself—to see if I could be independent, stand on my own, make my own way.

I lived with Aunt Sophia and Uncle Zygmunt and Dolek in an apartment they shared with a few other survivors. The three of them slept in one room and I slept in another, sharing a bed with another woman.

Business took my uncle away at all hours, and he always returned with something in his small portmanteau to eat or to wear or to put on a shelf, some object presumed to be "better than money."

The late-winter cold of Lvov mocked my pleasure in wearing the elegant, now-torn sandals Jan had given me, and my skin under a short-sleeved dress and thin jacket turned a mottled red and blue. Aunt Sophia presented me with a coat in reasonably good shape, and my uncle traded a pound of butter for a pair of heavy, peach-colored stockings. Dolek had two wool caps and offered to let me wear whichever one he didn't prefer at the time.

Still, I felt like an outsider. Often, when I came home from school at two or three in the afternoon, there would be leftovers from their dinner for me to eat. I'm sure they didn't mean to neglect me—there was still a war on and food was scarce—but I felt almost like a stranger.

Attendance at school in the morning, as in Czortkow, was followed by work in the afternoon at an army office. For once I knew the latest war news. When we heard that the Germans had finally been pushed out of Warsaw, we danced among the desks.

In Lvov I had neither school friends—the few Jewish students were very guarded—nor an escort from work. It exhilarated me at twilight to strike out on my own down unfamiliar streets and trust my sense of direction to land me, eventually, back at my aunt and uncle's apartment building. Yet it was a sad time for me. I felt lonely. I missed my mother and my brother. And I missed Jan.

One evening, Uncle Zygmunt's nephew arrived from Skala to have supper with us. At first he was quiet, shooting quick glances at me as he spooned his soup. He was about four years older than I, with heavy black hair and the insistent shadow of a beard made doubly dark by his bone-white skin. As we ate dessert, my aunt gestured to my uncle and Dolek to follow her out of the room.

The nephew told me he had lived through the war by remaining, day after day, one hayloft ahead of the Germans and Ukrainians. As he told me some incidents of flight I marveled at his luck. "Luck, yes—and this," he said, tapping his forehead. He invited me to go to the movies with him.

As we stepped out of the cinema lobby, he suggested that I come to his room "for tea." I told him I had school the next day. He took my elbow, saying, "Don't be a baby," and steered me in a direction that I knew did not lead to where I lived. I pulled away and walked off. He ran in front of me. "You think you're too good for me." He looked as if he was about to spit at me. "You had a *goy*. Why not me?"

The next morning my aunt set a bowl of porridge in front of me. "Did you have a good time last night?"

I said I had enjoyed the movie, a Russian picture with lots of galloping horses.

"Why did you tell him about Jan and me?"

My aunt sat down facing me. "Everybody knows. If he didn't hear it from me, he would hear it from someone else. Did you like him?"

I got up and gathered my books for school.

"Do you want to marry a *goy* who left school after the eighth grade? You can't tear yourself away from him?"

She gestured for me to sit down. "I'm saying this for your own good. He saved your life. Your parents' and Arthur's lives. So thank him. Finished. Do you have to marry him?" Her voice softened as she saw my defiance turning to tears.

"Why do you think I brought you to Lvov?"

So that was it. "Look," I said, inching toward the door, "I wouldn't marry him even if he was king of England."

She got up to make sure I'd hear her last words as I ran down the stairs. "A murderer! You want to marry the man who killed your father!"

Her words echoed in my head. She said them not as a question but as fact. What proof did she have? She wanted to spread poison on the hand that had saved me over and over again, a hand schooled in tenderness, a hand missing some fingers, a broad and calloused hand with a deep palm that fed me water when I was dying of thirst. Every time he touches you with that hand, she was saying, think of your father. Think, she was saying, of who you are.

Chapter Seventy

THE DAY JAN'S COUSIN ELENA arrived at the apartment to say that Jan was expected soon and to invite me to her house, I told my aunt I would not be home for dinner. After work, taking the can of preserved meat given me by an admirer at the office, I knocked on Elena's door. Blue-eyed, blond Elena and her husband owned a fairly large house with a big garden and a gazebo covered by grape vines. As I stood there, I looked forward to the warm weather when Jan and I would drink lemonade in the arbor, or Jan would repair some household object for Elena, and I . . . I pictured my books spread on the table as I did my homework.

I presumed Elena wanted me to help prepare a welcoming party for Jan, but when I saw her sorrowful face I became alarmed.

"No, nothing has happened to Jan," she said. She placed me in a chair and sat down next to me. "Not to him but . . ." She couldn't speak for a minute. Finally, after I comforted her for her undisclosed grief, she said, "Your mother, it's your mother."

"What? What happened to my mother? Is she hurt?"

"She's dead. She was killed in the forest."

I fainted. Before I opened my eyes I felt a pain in my side. I

must have bumped my hip on the table as I fell. Elena applied a
cold rag to my temple.

Elena's husband came in the door, followed by Jan.

He rushed over to me. I began to cry, and he took me in his
arms and rocked me. "What happened?" I asked. "Tell me what
happened."

Jan looked puzzled. Elena explained that I had fainted from
the shock of hearing my mother was dead.

"She's alive," he said. "I went to see her before I left and she
gave me this for you." He handed me a pair of worn but warm
slippers.

He saw that I didn't believe him. "It was a mix-up." This was
his story:

Once a month my mother went to the marketplace in Czortkow by wagon to sell tobacco leaves which she had bought from
farmers. The rich soil of the Ukraine was perfect for tobacco
culture. Merchants would dry the leaves, grind them up, and sell
the tobacco to cigarette makers.

One morning the previous week, as my mother was getting
ready to leave the house and catch a ride, Arthur began crying
and begged her not to go. She told him they would have nothing
to eat if she didn't go, but he made such a fuss that she stayed to
calm him. Then, an hour or two later, she went to the spot
where she usually managed to get a seat in a market-bound
wagon. The wagon she usually took had left. After waiting for
some time, she was about to give up and go home when a farmer
late for market agreed to let her ride in his wagon.

When they arrived in the square in Czortkow, an agitated
woman made the sign of the cross and said, "What, you're not
dead!" The *Banderowtzi* had waylaid the first wagon, the one my
mother usually rode in, killing the two Jewish women passengers,
plundering their goods, and letting the others go. Jan hesitated,
then said: "That's it." I could tell by his face there was more,
and I insisted he tell the rest. "They sliced off the women's
tongues and gouged out their eyes . . ."

Jan stopped speaking.

"Why did they think it was my mother?"

"One of the dead women was named Gottesfeld," he said. I knew the woman, one of "the other Gottesfelds."

Elena came over to me with a pillow to support my back. "I'm so sorry," she said. "When I heard 'Mrs. Gottesfeld,' I thought . . ."

For days I couldn't shake the after-blitz of shock. I wrote to my mother asking if Arthur had been told she was dead. Yes, she wrote back, but he was all right. When she returned and walked into the room, he told her she had to regard him as her savior and be grateful to him for the rest of her life because he had made her miss the first wagon.

Chapter Seventy-one

DURING THAT SPRING of 1945 in Lvov, as the war drew to an end, my aunt arranged Sunday teas and unearthed a string of eligible men for me to meet. It irked me to be expected to encourage these marriage-hungry men.

Jan was not welcome at my aunt and uncle's home. He had moved in with Elena and we met several times a week, but he was still under pressure to pay court to the Skala girl used as a cover when he was accused of being a "Jewish uncle."

Some Sunday mornings I took my schoolbooks to Elena's and told my aunt I was going to a girlfriend's house to study. Although I didn't return until nine or ten at night, she never asked what I had done that day. I would certainly not have told her that I had dinner at the home of Elena and her husband and then spent a few hours with Jan outdoors or in his room. She didn't know he was in Lvov until my mother mentioned it in a letter.

"Come to Cracow with us," Aunt Sophia said one evening as we were finishing supper.

I told her I couldn't leave school now, with only a few months left before I'd finish the last term and got my diploma.

"You can finish there," she said. She, Zygmunt, and Dolek

intended to work their way west to Paris. "You can come with us."

I told her that when I returned to Skala I would ask my mother if she and Arthur wanted to go to Cracow.

"Not your mother and Arthur," my uncle said. "Just you."

I had been making plans to bring my mother and Arthur to Lvov. There were rumors afloat that the Jews of Skala and the surrounding area were going to be shipped off to Siberia.

"I'm going back to Skala," I said. I took my plate and fork and put them in the sink. "Thanks for your offer. But I prefer being with my mother and brother even if it means going to Siberia. I belong with them."

I ran to my room. Dolek came in. "What's wrong?" he asked as I cried into my pillow.

"Nothing. I'm going back to Skala. I'm crying because I'm so happy."

When I told Jan that my aunt and uncle were going to Cracow and I back to Skala, he betrayed no sign of being upset. "After Easter," he said, "you can come back here and finish school. I can find a room for you in a house near Elena's."

"I'm not coming back to Lvov," I said. "From now on I'm staying with my mother and Arthur." It meant I was one semester short of graduating from high school, but I felt I had no choice.

Back in Skala, I found my mother despondent because there were no *matzos* available and no Passover celebration. Nevertheless, she showed how pleased she was to have me home by declining my offer to scrub the floor. "Sit," she said, "and read a book." Then after a minute she said, "Well, on second thought, if you could patch this sheet," and she held up a tattered piece of fabric. "See if you can mend this so you won't have to sleep on the bare mattress."

The pair of heavy irons borrowed from a neighbor had to stand on the stove for ages before they sizzled hot enough to flatten coarse fabric. The steamed-linen smell from the crazily patched sheet I was ironing on and off melded with the odor of stewing onions from my mother's cooking.

I wandered to the window and saw Jan coming up the street. Now that I'd left Lvov, he had, too, and was living again in Czortkow. When Arthur saw Jan, he jumped up, ran out to him, and held his hand as they walked to the door.

My mother sat Jan down and insisted that he try a plate of her "chicken" soup, which earned its name only by the grace of a few chicken feet that had strayed through it. Jan pronounced it first class, and I had to admit later that my mother was an expert counterfeiter.

We speculated on how long it would take the Allies to defeat the Japanese. My mother said he must come tomorrow to eat the carrots he had brought, which she had not been able to afford.

If we had been able to have a Passover *seder*, and Jan and I were married, would Jan have been there? Or would my mother have banished him from the house? A *goy*, son-in-law or not, I could not picture at our *seder*. But then, there was Jan's presence in our family as I had witnessed it: my father's and Jan's heads bent down to examine a plan for a hideout, Jan carrying my mother up the ladder to the hiding place in his barn, Arthur riding on Jan's shoulders—all these and a thousand other scenes of Jan with us were stored in a big box called "the war." Now the box was hidden under a sheet like the one I was ironing.

None of us could bear to speak of my father. The rudder of the boat had sunk to the bottom of the river.

Chapter Seventy-two

J AN INVITED ME to Easter dinner at his cousin Irena's house. His mother and sister would not be there. After he left, my mother said she was surprised I had agreed to go to the Easter celebration.

"Why?"

"If the girl he's supposed to be courting finds out you were invited and not her, there'll be trouble." She had not entirely relinquished also the theory that Dzsisiak had murdered my father.

"Don't worry," I said. "Jan wouldn't invite me if it wasn't all right."

She stopped working for a moment. I looked at her and saw a gaunt-faced woman who had no use for her old headache bands, a woman determined to survive with her children and make sure they would have a decent life to look forward to.

"Watch yourself," she said. "Watch yourself when you go there."

Irena's small house was very clean, with whitewashed walls and a table large enough to seat all the guests. All but Irena, who had black braids, were blond. The men were mostly heavily muscled except for Irena's shoemaker husband, who was short and skinny. The women wore blouses and jackets embroidered in the folk style.

I marveled at the variety of food on the heaping platters. The men, as they ate the soup, hunched down to it with the concentration of peasants just in from working in the fields. I was reminded of Marynka as I watched a woman search her mouth with her fingers and withdraw a string of meat from her teeth.

"Don't you like blood pudding?" Jan's cousin asked.

I assured her I did and pretended to spoon it up with a broad display of relish. But I couldn't eat it or pigs' feet, either.

Everyone but Jan, who had never been a drinker, and I tossed back glass after glass of vodka. They joked and gossiped. Although the frequent toasts of vodka surely helped the general conviviality, this was obviously a family whose members liked each other.

Jan had seated me next to him and kept one arm around my shoulders protectively until he had to cut his meat. When he replaced his arm, I wriggled to indicate that he should remove it. He ignored my hint. To these people who meant so much to him he was saying, "This is my girl," just as he had done so many times when my life had been in jeopardy. I'm sure he wanted to make a statement to his family that it was I who was his girlfriend, not the Ukrainian woman he was still officially courting. Still, I didn't like his showing people I didn't know that he owned me, and I felt uncomfortable.

Jan became so engrossed in an anecdote he was telling that he removed his arm from my shoulders, and I managed to move my chair back to escape the radiating heat from the stoked bodies. After several more hours, during which the eating and drinking never abated, and parochial anecdotes and references to family stories swirled in and out of my ears, I dozed off in my chair.

"Do you want me to take you home?" Jan asked.

"She must be bored by us," someone said.

"No," another relative answered. "She passed out." Lots of laughter.

I told Jan I felt fine and that he needn't walk me home. Stepping briskly along the streets, I wondered if they were telling me something by the pressure of their squeezes as we shook hands to say good-bye.

Chapter Seventy-three

O F THE FIFTY JEWS who had trickled back to Skala, some were conscripted by the Russians, and some, like my uncle and aunt and Dolek, migrated west. About thirty of us were left. One day in May, when the *Banderowtzi* killed a Jew walking on the street, we could no longer ignore the signal that it was time to depart.

Skala, with most of the area which had been Galicia in Austria-Hungary before World War I, was slated to become part of the Soviet Ukraine in accordance with various postwar deals. The Polish government-in-exile and the Soviet government signed an agreement to permit non-Ukrainians—ethnic Poles and Jews—to leave for Poland. Skala's Jews decided to band together and go to the recently liberated section of western Poland called Upper Silesia. The Russians agreed to provide a train for us.

Ulanowski, who was Polish, also decided to leave for Silesia with his wife and two sons. So did Moizesevich. He was Armenian, but his wife, whom he'd married before the war, was Polish, the widow of a major in the army. Sidor could have left as well, but not Marynka, who was a Ukrainian, and he chose to stay behind with her. Jan, of course, was not eligible to leave, and he said he was going to try to get false Polish papers and join us in Silesia.

We had a few weeks to get ready, which meant converting the goods and provisions we had managed to amass in the year since the Liberation into items that could be carried in a pack. Since we had very little—a few pots, an old table and a few chairs, two beds, and a large zinc washtub, plus a few articles of clothing—conversion was not difficult. In fact, my mother enjoyed reselling the items for which she had bargained so skillfully and buying foodstuffs.

She baked crackers and loaves of bread, which she dried, and hunted in the market for a good supply of kasha, which she cooked in big pots on the stove, and of flour and sugar. She rendered fat into lard and packed it into crocks sealed with wax. She also made and sealed jars of jam. All these foods were designed to last a long time.

My mother's memories of hunger and starvation sanctioned any expedient short of the seriously criminal to keep them from reappearing. She came home one day with a container of walnuts. "They were sitting on a window sill as I passed," she said. "Such a shame to let them dry up."

"Whose window sill?"

"Who knows? I don't know who lives there now. It was once a Jewish window sill." The shrug of her shoulders, the tilt of her head, the *moue* of her mouth combined to say: Let them come for me, my children must eat.

"How are we going to carry it all?" I asked.

"We'll carry it," she said. "If we don't have something to eat, they'll have to carry *us* somewhere."

Day after day I debated whether I should go to Jan's cousin Irena to leave word for him that we were going or should simply leave and then write him. He hadn't come to see me since Easter. He hadn't written or sent a message.

Five days before our scheduled departure, Sidor dropped in to bring us some bread. He asked about Jan. I said I hadn't seen him for a while. He stopped fitting a cardboard sole into Arthur's shoe and gave me a long look. "Is he getting married?"

"I don't know," I said. With Sidor I didn't have to pretend I didn't care. Sidor said he would come by and bring some vodka before we left. "You'll take it with you," he said. "It's as good as money."

My mother gave him our large zinc washtub. I could see that he didn't want it but was too polite to refuse.

"Do you expect me to carry it home on my head?" he asked.

"Marynka will want it," my mother said. He promised to bring his wagon next time. He had a new, strong horse, and he wanted us to see it.

Sidor had barely closed the door behind him before my mother burst into tears. "We have nothing to give him." I couldn't keep my own tears back. After all the promises to Sidor and Marynka, we were giving them a washtub! And Paris? There was no way of knowing whether Aunt Esther and her family were still alive.

"Tonight we'll dig again," I said to my mother as I brought her a glass of water.

Soon after we came out of hiding, my mother and I had gone back to the yard behind our old house one dark night to dig for the silver items my father had buried there. But we couldn't find a trace of even one. Perhaps I'd still been too weak and hadn't dug deep enough.

My mother brightened at my suggestion. "Yes, I'm sure Papa buried six silver *schnapps* glasses near the big tree."

We set out at about three in the morning. A quarter-moon shed more light than I wanted, since it was a clear night. The people who had taken over our house could beat us or shoot us for trespassing. I didn't care.

I carried a pick in a sack so that no light would reflect from the blade. My mother had a pot lid to use as a trowel. We worked until the sky paled during first light. My mother, too exhausted to continue, sat down on a pile of earth. "It's no use," she said. "Someone was here before us."

I began to refill the last hole. Sidor would receive no payment. He had never asked for any. Even a sack full of silver objects couldn't begin to recompense him for what he'd done to save us. But Marynka would have liked the silver *schnapps* glasses. Under my breath I cursed the thief who had stolen them.

Chapter Seventy-four

E ARLY IN THE MORNING, two days later, I slipped out of the house before anyone else was awake. Irena had brought a message from Jan the day before: he wanted me to meet him in her garden at eleven.

As I walked out the door, I felt the kind of May warmth that erases the last vestiges of winter chill and guarantees blue skies for the entire summer.

Soon I'd be leaving Skala for good, and I wanted to take a farewell tour of all my old walks. My first stop was the Hebrew school, an empty shell, and its library, which had been totally ransacked. The Germans had taken away whatever the Russians had left behind—all the books were gone. On the road to the count's estate, which was garnished by late-spring flowers, the turmoil of feelings that used to attack me as I went to deliver sweaters to the manager wavered over me like a dark cloud.

The cloud darkened as I took a walk up to the Turkish Tower, as I'd often done before the war with Lotka or Zhenia and sometimes with Izio. My two best friends were dead, Shimek was dead, and as for Izio, I hadn't seen him after the Liberation.

As I sat and looked at the thick stones of the fort and down over the newly green countryside to the river and beyond, an overflow of tears took me past these losses to the question that came so often. Why me? Why had I been spared? Kicking stones on the way down, which was always much swifter than the ascent, I marveled that the road had not altered, that the flowers still grew in profuse clumps, that the duplicitous landscape gave no hint of what had happened here during the last four years.

Passing the public park and its bandstand, where I'd often listened to military marches, and the Cukernia cafe, where Grandfather Azriel had bought me chocolates and other treats, I ended up at the railroad station and saw the stationmaster, the same grandly mustachioed one who had been on duty for as long as I could remember. He was standing on the platform with the same red flag signaling an approaching train with wide-armed strokes that had a different message for me than when I was a young girl. I used to think it meant, Stop, stop in Skala, the best place in the world. Now, as the train, an express, passed through, I realized he must have been sending a different message, one saying, Go, pass Skala by, go west . . .

I walked back to the central square, speeding up as I passed the houses of former classmates from the Polish school. On my last day in Skala, I didn't want to come face to face with any of them—too often since the Liberation I had heard their incredulous and disappointed words, "So you've come back!"

The houses on the main avenue where we'd lived were deserted, their doors and windows gone. They seemed to totter, unrooted in the ground.

Skala seemed like a ghost town.

In the debris of one house, I found a small, badly torn book, the only evidence that people had once lived there. I put it in my pocket and walked on.

When I got to Irena's, Jan was waiting for me in the gazebo.

Jumping up, he rushed toward me and kissed me and held me, and during the time in his arms I thought, Yes, it's all right, we're together, nothing has changed.

He held my hand as Irena brought us bread and cheese and strawberries. He said he had moved permanently to Czortkow and was working as a carpenter or ditch digger, whatever day labor he could get: "Sometimes I look up from the muck I'm standing in and see a high school girl pass with books in her arms and I think of our afternoon walks."

I reminded him of the time in Czortkow when I had forgotten my books behind a rock and how we had to walk back many kilometers to get them. "Yes, and you looked behind the wrong rock and began to cry because they weren't there."

We laughed and he stroked my hand. "The *Banderowtzi*," I said, "could have found us, and that would have been it."

"Not for us. We lead charmed lives." Jan leaned back on the wooden bench. "I'm going with that girl . . ." He looked at me as if by looking deep into my eyes he could discover how I felt. "I go to see her, but it doesn't mean anything."

I nodded in a comprehending yes.

"I'm not getting married. I promise you that. Not till the war is over." Did he mean to her or to me, I wondered. I decided it didn't matter today, not on this fine spring day.

He told me how ugly Silesia was, that everything reeked of coal dust, even the grass. "Tuberculosis," he said. "That's what you have to guard against." He put his arms around me again and began to cry. His warm tears soaked my neck and collar. For a while I managed to hold back, and then I cried too. We'd never see each other again, that's what today's sunshine was all about: a blind, a screen so that I would not be able to look at the loneliness ahead. I felt I was leaving part of myself behind.

The flint floor of the gazebo served as couch, a reminder that our love came out of hiding in harsh places and lived on stone ground.

Later, as we walked around the garden, Jan stopped to cut an early rose for me. We talked about the garden's budding trees, and then he led me back to the gazebo. From an inside pocket of his jacket he drew a folded piece of velvet cloth and put it in my hand. Something hard inside. A gold ring, a plain band of gold.

He gave me a kiss and put it on my finger. He looked into my eyes with that intensity of his, a wordlessness that spoke of too many words, and then he turned and walked away.

Chapter Seventy-five

I LOOKED FOR JAN at the station the day we left. I knew it was a working day and that Czortkow was 45 kilometers away, but still I half-expected him to see me off.

The commotion of departure from our birthplace, from the dead we were leaving there, crystallized into keeping an attentive eye on the bundles at our feet. The Russians had sent cattle cars without roofs, not cars with seats. "Maybe they will bring us luck," someone said. We had heard confirmed stories of the *Banderowtzi* stopping passenger trains, dragging Jews out and shooting them.

Just as I began to load our things in the car, Irena tapped me on the shoulder. She said that Jan was sorry he couldn't come but had sent me a little present to say good-bye—and she put a small box in my hand. I didn't know what to say. She shook my hand hard and left.

I walked around the corner of the station to open Jan's gift. The box itself was covered in prettily patterned, somewhat faded paper. Inside it were five gold coins.

We hadn't been told where in Silesia we were headed, only that the trip wouldn't take more than a day. It took four weeks.

The train had wheels but they hardly ever turned. Most of the time we were becalmed at a siding or a station. After rolling along for fifteen minutes one day, we would sit derailed in an adjoining field for the next three. Once, after many days' travel, we stopped at a station, and everyone fought to get to the water basin or the rain barrel. Several times we heard horses' hooves after the train had ground to a halt, and I was sure the *Banderow-tzi* were coming for us.

Some people ran away, saying it was a doomed train. Others fell sick, and a few died. My mother's stash of food was a lifesaver on that four-week journey.

One day in the fourth week, my mother fell into a fit of crying from which I couldn't distract her. She crawled around on all fours, pushing the straw on the floor from side to side. She refused to tell me what she was looking for.

Finally she stopped and didn't move at all. Looking at her, I saw what I must look like. Her hair stuck together in clumps and the blotched skin of her face reminded me of the ground of Sidor's hen yard. Our clothes were filthy and had hardened from dried perspiration.

She spoke slowly: "I lost it. I'll never forgive myself. How could I lose it?" And she began to search the straw again.

Finally she told me what "it" was: Jan's gold ring. I had given it to her because it fit her finger. She had wanted to wear it because her own marriage band had been traded away ages ago, and looking at it reminded her of my father.

I asked her when she'd lost the ring. She wasn't sure. The ring had somehow gotten stuck on a hook when the train lurched forward, she said. It had probably slipped off when she pulled her finger off the hook.

I was upset. "You could have lost a finger." She came up with another theory: "Maybe it slipped off when I was putting preserves on the bread. Then it must be here." She searched some more.

I tried to hold her. "Ma, forget the ring. We don't need it. It doesn't matter." She pushed me away.

I blamed myself for not having worn it around my neck on a string, thereby saving my mother this pain.

I had been conflicted over the ring, which is probably why I was so eager to give it to my mother when she asked me for it. I felt uncomfortable about the ring from the start, not knowing where it came from, or more specifically, whose it had been, and also what it symbolized for Jan. Jan did not tell me where he'd gotten the ring, and it hadn't occurred to me to inquire, but when my mother asked, I saw immediately that she thought of it as stolen goods: a Jewish ring, perhaps, or from the finger of a dead German or Ukrainian, like the chopped-off ones we had seen on the battlefield. Whether Jan had taken it from a corpse or bought it from someone who had, came to the same thing. I regretted not giving the ring back right there in the gazebo. It was the May weather that had befuddled me.

At the time I did not realize that the ring was a wedding band, and that Jan was trying to imply something by putting it on my finger. According to old folk beliefs and medieval Christian practice in Eastern Europe, a man could marry a woman simply by saying "I marry thee" and putting a ring on her finger. No witnesses were required, as they were in Jewish marriage ceremonies.

My mother's voice shook me out of my thoughts. "Jan gave you the ring for all of us. With it we could have bought papers and gone to Paris. Now we have nothing."

I hadn't shown the five gold coins to my mother. Now I gave them to her. They eased her upset, but every once in a while she again started reproaching herself for losing the ring.

The train stopped. As usual, we were in the middle of nowhere. Then someone said, "I smell coal." Yes, we were in coal country. "When everyone gets out, I'm going through the straw one strand at a time," my mother said. "I have a feeling it's still in this car."

But I knew the ring was gone forever. Gone with our house, our beautiful candlesticks, the ring we'd given Derewienko, the buried schnapps glasses and tea holders, the shimmering silk dresses and Parisian suits. Gone with the life we'd had before the war. Gone with the aunts and uncles, the cousins, the friends. Of everyone and everything we'd had in Skala, only Jan remained. And now I had lost his ring.

I told myself that losing it didn't mean that Jan was lost too. The rose he had given me in the garden, that I still had. I'd pressed it into the small, torn book I found in Skala on my last walk through town.

We arrived at the barracks of the DP camp in Bytom with the little book, a sack with what was left of the food we'd taken along on the train, Grandfather Azriel's old coat, and a comb made useless by our tangled hair.

And the five gold coins.

VII

Bytom

(August–December 1945)

Chapter Seventy-six

J AN HAD PREDICTED how bleak Bytom would be, but nothing had prepared me for the black skin on every house, every street, and even on the children as they played in the coal-smutted alleys. The black grass in the park didn't discourage the pigeons, who were a shade lighter. There weren't many of them, and they were never offered food. There was none to spare.

There was very little to buy in the shops other than glass objects which sported the Bytom insignia emblazoned in black, red, and gold: a man with a pickaxe chipping at a wall of coal, and joined to it, a German eagle ascendant. Bytom had been part of Germany both before and during the war.

The DP camp consisted of wooden barracks with large halls which served as our dormitories. Day after day, people lay on their cots without moving, small islands of despair and sorrow marooned by exhaustion, by malnutrition, and by illness. Some committed suicide. Others—including Ulanowski and Moisezevich and their families, with whom we stayed in touch in the camp and shared advice and information—left as soon as they could.

My mother, a tireless provider in Skala, was disoriented by

the trip, the camp, and the unfamiliar people, and contented herself with monitoring Arthur and talking to other survivors.

The talent for lassitude I had cultivated while in hiding worked against me in Bytom. Keeping busy was the only antidote. The grapevine served as newspaper. With leads from my mother, I learned where to apply for the myriad necessities, from soap to exit visas. My fluency in German helped my daily trading activities. Once a week I stood in line at the offices of the Joint Distribution Committee for our food package, setting aside the bare minimum we needed for ourselves and using the rest for barter. If there was flour I converted some of it into fat, tinned meat into bread, and so on. We supplemented our meager diet with what remained of the food we had brought with us from Skala.

We got a letter from Aunt Sophia in Cracow. She wrote that she'd heard from Aunt Esther in Paris. All the members of our family were alive. When they got my father's postcard, sent before the *aktsia*, they fled to Vichy and then went into hiding. The postcard had saved their lives, Esther wrote.

Aunt Sophia added that she'd told Aunt Esther where we were and that she, Uncle Zygmunt, and Dolek were leaving for Salzburg in Austria.

I also got a letter from Jan. The badly mauled envelope had preceded us to Bytom, arriving in half the time it had taken us. No word from us for so long had worried him.

I knew I should answer, a duty that would occur to me as I was trudging across Bytom on some errand and promptly forgot when I got back. Jan and Skala and all that had happened in the last three years, vivid as ever, I kept wrapped up and slung over my back where I could ignore them. They were no use to me in Bytom.

Chapter Seventy-seven

I KNEW THE FIRST PRIORITY was to find us a place to live. I finally found a room in a rundown workers' neighborhood. At the market, an old woman speaking very poor Polish had asked if I'd be interested in the exchange of a room for an occasional bag of flour. It was in an apartment, four flights up, with no electricity and with one toilet in the hall for the tenants of the entire landing. The rutted linoleum on the floor tripped me as I entered.

When my mother, Arthur, and I arrived there, we found we would be sharing the place not only with its tenant, Miss Klampt, but also with her six cats. Miss Klampt looked like one of those old maids in a French movie—ageless and sexless.

"With you I can speak German," she said to me. Now that Silesia was part of Poland, she was afraid to speak German in public and her Polish was terrible. But our real value as her tenants was the weekly *Joint* package, stretching now to feed four humans plus the cats—all of whom were starving.

Miss Klampt slept in the kitchen with the cats, and we had a little room overlooking a dingy courtyard that even in summer sent up clouds of black dust when I stuck my head out the window for air. Earlier in the year, while in the hiding place, I would have done anything for that privilege, a thought that did little to make things better. My mother reverted to her Skala cleaning mania and her headaches, leaving me to do all the cooking.

Arthur was pleased with the cats. He had only one friend who came to play with him and was not permitted to play with the children in the courtyard. He spent most of his time at the window, watching them. My mother made a cover for the window sill to protect his forearm, but coal motes flew into his eyes and mouth. "Everything tastes sooty," he said.

Miss Klampt was an excellent seamstress but lacked clientele because fabric was unobtainable. She offered to sew a new outfit for me in order to attract a husband who would "solve all your problems." Her regret that she had not been rescued by marriage did not extend to children. "Cats are not as great a burden," she said. From Grandfather Azriel's black shiny coat that my mother did not have the heart to barter away in Skala before we left, Miss Klampt made me a suit.

One day I managed to talk the driver of a Russian truck transporting machinery to Breslau into giving me a place among the crates. At the market I had no trouble exchanging items from *Joint* packages for clothes. Late in the day, dressed in everything I had bought—a housedress for my mother, pants that could be cut down for Arthur, a man's jacket to sell, and some men's tricot shirts—I wangled a ride back to Bytom in a truck carrying five Russian soldiers. My bizarre ensemble did nothing to discourage each one in turn from sitting next to me and kneading his hands over my body, which was insulated from sensation by the many layers of fabric. Eventually vodka, heat, and rocking from the bumpy roads put them to sleep. I fought against sleep, and when I finally jumped off in Bytom, vowed not to take such a risk again.

It turned out to be a profitable trip. In the market in Bytom, my mother got more than a week's worth of food for the man's jacket and shirts. I kept one knitted tricot shirt, which Miss Klampt dyed light blue and made into a blouse for me. It looked smart with my glossy black suit, and Miss Klampt predicted I could have my pick of beaus when I wore it.

Chapter Seventy-eight

WINTER WAS COMING, and I was feeling more and more desperate. We had no money for coal or warm clothes for Arthur, and there were no jobs. I looked forward to snow, for a white cloud to cover the blackness of Bytom, but knew it would make my sandals, little enough protection during rain, useless.

Arthur would go out early in the morning and stand on the long bread line, clutching ration stamps and money, but he often came back empty-handed. "No more bread," he'd say, as if it were as natural as saying water is wet, and then he'd go to the window and sit there without moving for the rest of the day.

My mother, ill with bronchitis, needed medicine, which I couldn't afford. I nursed her as best I could, but her spirit appeared more damaged than her body. When she insisted on going to a spa to recover, I saw that she had retreated into a prewar world of her own. Miss Klampt, afraid she would catch my mother's illness, threatened to evict us.

Aunt Sophia and Uncle Zygmunt, writing from Salzburg, promised to send help when they got to Paris, but we heard nothing from them all fall.

Finally, I broke down and answered Jan's letter, writing how much I missed him. The minute I mailed the letter, I started to feel anxious. Did I really want to see him again? I don't know—one day I missed him, and the next day I wanted to run away from him. He was the first man in my life, he was my security. He had saved my life, but should I sacrifice it—should I give a life for a life? Should I give up my dream of studying medicine in Paris and become a Ukrainian housewife, cooking blood puddings and pigs' feet, and having Easter dinners where everybody got drunk? We were so different; how could we be happy together?

Each day I wished the letter would get lost in the mail, and yet I ran to the mailbox to see if a reply had arrived. It came on a morning when my mother's fever had returned and we had enough bread to last for only two more meals.

The letter carrier, who was used to seeing me wait for his delivery, handed me two envelopes. I opened the one with the French stamps first and found in the fold of my Aunt Esther's letter a fifty-dollar bill. Now we could go to Paris.

Jan's letter described the steps he was taking to get false Polish papers so he could join me in Bytom. So far, the papers hadn't come through.

"I know you want me as much as I want you," he wrote, "but I don't know if you'll have me." I groped for a seat on the stairs.

I thought of all the times he'd held me through the night as I trembled with fear, how he took care of me when I was so sick, how we had shared our secrets in his barn and in our bed of straw in Sidor's attic. I thought of how gentle he was to me when we made love—how we had known each other for a year before he touched me, how I loved his rough and bony hands caressing me as the sun poured in. "You're so beautiful," he'd said. I thought of how he'd cried when he gave me the rose from his cousin's garden, an early rose of spring. I knew that no one would ever love me as much as he did.

My feelings for him—impossible to untangle from my deep feelings of gratitude—weighted on one end of the scale. And then, on the other end, I saw the image of a baby, my baby, the child I would have with Jan if we married, a baby with the face of my father—and a cross hanging from his neck.

How could I have children who would not be Jews? How could

I betray my promise to my father, made when we were hiding in the chicken coop, that my children would read Shakespeare and go to Hebrew school?

If Jan came to Bytom and began a life here, and I stayed with him, we would never get out of Poland—assuming Jan would be able to get false papers, which was next to impossible. Nor could I return to Skala to live with him there, a lone Jew among Ukrainians, who hated and had murdered my people. We would never be able to leave either place, we would never go to Paris or anywhere else. We and our children would live out our lives and die in this land of death.

How could I condemn my babies to grow up in Poland or the Ukraine, the graveyard for millions of Jews? No, not a graveyard, for there were no graves. The Jews had been burned to ashes, and the ashes had turned to dust which was in the air we breathed and the water we drank. It was like the coal dust of Bytom.

I saw myself holding a baby to my breast, and my breast and the baby were black with the ashes of their murdered relatives. Black milk came out of my breast. My baby coughing like Wolf and Malcia's daughter when she was ill with diphtheria in the hiding place under the warehouse during the *aktsia*. Jan holding the baby and crying as the child turned stiff in his arms and broke in two like a dry twig, then turned to dust and became part of the dust in the air and the water . . .

I went inside and sat down next to my mother on the bed and cooled her brow with a cloth. Again, I saw one side of the scale descend and then the other, a seesaw motion that caused me to fall into an anxious, terrified daze.

Chapter Seventy-nine

ARTHUR TAPPED ME ON THE HEAD, jolting me out of my terror. "Get up," he said. A man I had never seen before stood at the door. I was still clutching the two letters.

He introduced himself as Israel, a good friend of my parents from Skala. "For old times' sake and because you're such a beautiful girl," he said, "I'm going to do it for nothing."

"Do what?"

"Send you a nice man who wants to marry you."

The next morning, when my mother's fever went down a little, I told her of the matchmaker's visit.

"It won't cost anything," she said. "The husband pays anyway."

"But I don't want to get married."

"With nothing in the house to eat, you can afford to say no?" At least her mind wasn't wandering. I told her about the fifty dollars. She closed her eyes and turned away.

I found a man who could arrange three places on an illegal transport to Paris. I gave him the fifty dollars and promised we'd be ready to leave on short notice. In the meantime, I decided to humor my mother. I stopped at Israel's place to leave a message that he could send the "nice man" to visit me some evening.

When I came home from my frantic trip, jubilant that we were slated to leave in two days, I found my mother delirious. I saw she needed medicine and good food, not a train journey. I ran to get the fifty dollars back. "Too late," the man said, "but I'll consider it a deposit for another transport."

Israel sent three men in rapid succession, and for each visit my mother insisted on getting dressed up, despite a persistent low-grade fever. I went to the movies with one, on a stroll with another, and to tea with the third. I answered their questions with small gestures and few words. All three proposed.

I picked the one who took me to the movies. His name was Joseph. He was handsome—blond and very slim, a year older than I, and very religious. He prayed in the morning, ate only kosher food, and observed the Shabbat.

Joseph was very sweet and gentle, and had a quality of innocence that appealed to me. He looked like a little deer who had nobody to care for him and needed protection; indeed, he had lived like an animal for the two years he was in hiding underground, and had almost forgotten how to talk.

He was originally from a little *shtetl* next to Skala—our grandparents probably knew each other. Joseph's mother had died when he was eight years old. His father, a descendant of the famous Rabbi Yom Tov Lippmann Heller, was a wheat dealer who, like Grandfather Jakob, lost everything during the Depression.

After Joseph's sister made *aliyah* in the mid-1930s, his father followed. He left Joseph with a married sister, hoping to have all the children join him later. The outbreak of the war made this impossible.

After the Liberation, Joseph ran away when he got word that the Ukrainians were looking for him because he knew what stolen property had belonged to Jews in the *shtetl*. He fled from city to city, first to Czernowitz, from there to Bucharest, and then to Budapest.

The youngest and only survivor of his siblings, he had nobody and was very lonely. Learning that an old friend of his family had survived and was living in Bytom, he decided to find him.

The old friend, a fervent Zionist, had been a lawyer before 1939 and was one of my teachers at the Russian high school in Borszczow.

Joseph told this friend that he was lonely and wanted to get married. The friend sent Israel the matchmaker to see him, and Israel introduced him to three girls. Two of them he didn't like. I was the third.

Two days after we met, Joseph told me he wanted to marry me. He promised to give me a wonderful life, to provide well for me, and he swore I would study medicine and become a doctor. He also promised to take care of my mother and my brother— unlike Zygmunt's nephew, who had once said to me, "I like you, but I don't want to take your mother and your brother with us." It was very important for me to stay with my mother and Arthur and not be separated from them again.

When Joseph asked people about me, he was told that I was a very nice girl, intelligent, educated, and from a fine family, but that I'd had an affair with a *goy*. "You know," he said to me, "if you tell me that you're a virgin, I'll buy you the nicest Persian lamb coat." I told him, "You can save yourself the coat." He said nothing more and never asked me about Jan, not then and not ever, and I respected him for this.

I told my mother I liked him. "Are you crazy?" she said. "You know him for two days and you tell me you want to marry him?" My father had courted my mother for five years and I wanted to get married after two days, but those were different times.

We were engaged a week after we met. I remember my father saying that if I survived, this was all that mattered. His wish had come true.

Having lost both my father and Jan, I needed a man as quickly as possible, so we married at once.

At the engagement party, my mother sat on Miss Klampt's sofa with her arm around Arthur, whose new shoes, a gift from my fiancé, tapped a tune on the floor.

It irked me that money was being spent on a party when we didn't have enough for basic necessities. "It's wasted money," I told her.

"I paid for it and I think it's worth it," she answered.

"You? How?"

"The gold coins." Jan's coins! The coins had been a last resort, to be used only in case of mortal danger. My mother realized that that was over now because I was getting married and my husband would take care of us. I thought of the gold necklace I had once seen around the neck of a woman whose sooty face and neck dripped sweat and bathed the necklace in it, and how the gold looked as drab as lead.

Jan wasn't in the room, but I felt his hand entwined with mine, as it had been so many times when we walked or sat or lay in the dark on the brink of something. I felt his right hand, a large hand which easily accommodated mine, and I remembered the feel of the callouses on the ridge below the fingers—something strange to me at first because the men and boys I knew, my father and Shimek, had soft hands, whereas Jan's were strong and bony. I remembered his left hand and the way I used to grasp the three fingers, my hand making up for the two missing digits, our hands an entity, a sufficiency of holding, a melding—like a marriage.

Now Jan's gold was paving the road to my marriage with a stranger.

Jan's gold flowed down our gullets and those of our guests, and the herring and chicken and cake it bought tasted and smelled foreign to me, as if strange oils and spices had been used during their cooking. The schnapps, too, had the flavor of a fruit I'd never eaten.

As the guests whom my mother had scraped together—anyone with a remote connection to Skala—gave toast after toast for a fruitful union and a long life, Jan's coins filled our stomachs with manna and I tried to feel happy.

In a corner of the room, his last letter lay unanswered in my little torn book, next to the rose he had given me in Skala on our last day together.

Postscript

J OSEPH AND I MARRIED in January, 1946 and lived in Budapest, Vienna, Munich, Berlin and Holland before settling in New York. We had a son and two daughters, and, as of this writing, eight grandchildren.

Joseph died in 1986.

I never got to Paris to study medicine. I studied history of art at Columbia University, and philosophy and literature at the New School for Social Research in New York. I received B.A. and M.A. degrees in psychology from the New School.

My mother settled in New York in 1951, where she remarried.

She died, age 82, in 1982.

Arthur lives in New York City.

We never found out who had murdered my father.

Attempts to locate Sidor and Jan immediately following the war failed. Through the efforts of friends who maintain relationships in Ukraine, I received word in the summer of 1995 that Hania, Sidor's daughter is alive and living in Skala. Her parents

have died, as has Jan. After fifty-three years, plans for a reunion
with Hania Irena Sidorovna are now in progress.

F.G.H.
New York City
September, 1995